# A COVENANT

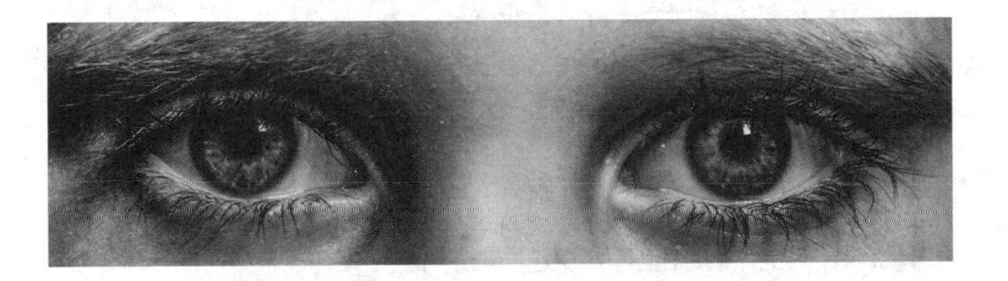

# WITH MY EYES

BOB SORGE

Oasis House
Kansas City, Missouri

A COVENANT WITH MY EYES

Published by Oasis House
PO Box 522
Grandview, MO 64030-0522
816-767-8880



Editors: Katie Hebbert and Edie Mourey
Cover designer: Joel Sorge
Typesetter: Dale Jimmo



Printed in the United States of America
ISBN: 978-1-937725-21-1
Library of Congress Control Number: 2013939761

For information on all Bob's books, see page 144.

www.oasishouse.com

**TO MY SON, MICHAEL**

I have watched the choices you've made. You've chosen consecration, abandonment to God's heart, and obedience to His call. You have honored your eye covenant with God, and He in turn has helped you. I'm grateful to Him that I can dedicate this book to you. May the grace of God enable you to share in a Revelation 14:4 company that is undefiled and follows the Lamb wherever He goes. Michael, call a generation to wholehearted love for Jesus—which is what an eye covenant is all about.

## GIVING OF THANKS

This book was a collaborative effort. I knew it was more than I could write alone, so I enlisted a small army to help. Special thanks goes to the following for their fantastic input into this book.

Katie Hebbert, Jennifer Roberts, Marci Sorge, Tracey Sliker, David Sliker, Corey Russell, Michael Sorge, Tracey Bickle, Sarah McNulty, Micah Rose Emerson, Benji Nolot, Anna Sorge, Marie Grotte, Hollie Carney, Nicola Walsh, Jeff Ell, Chris Wood, Joan Wood, Robert G. Smith, Joseph Zwanziger, Dale Anderson, Paul Johansson, Penn Clark, Matt Dawson, Josh Cole, Daniel Juster, Billy Humphrey, Dave Belles, Evan Beenhouwer, Sophia Beenhouwer, Mike Rizzo, James Crum, Kristen Williams, Sylvia Evans, David Kelso, Rebecca Myers, Rhonda Hughey, Michele Cole, Edie Mourey, Rosey Andrews, Eileen Tiberio, Linda Bloemberg, Kelly Spyker, Brenda Bravatty, Erik Eskelund, Tami Eskelund, and Kelsey Bohlender.

## CONTENTS

# PART ONE
# Introducing the Covenant

See how an eye covenant stops temptation from gaining access to your mind and heart.

## ONE

# "You've Never Actually Done It"

*The maiden was of beautiful form and pleasing appearance (Est. 2:7, Rotherham).*

**Sex.**

This book is about sex.

On the one hand, that gets our attention. We're interested. But at the same time, it makes us cringe slightly. "Where is this going? Will it be uncomfortable or awkward?"

We wince a bit at the mention of sex because of the blow Adam and Eve suffered in the garden of Eden.

> So when the woman saw that the tree was good for food, that it was pleasant to the eyes, and a tree desirable to make one wise, she took of its fruit and ate. She also gave to her husband with her, and he ate. Then the eyes of both of them were opened, and they knew that they were naked; and they sewed fig leaves together and made themselves coverings (Gen. 3:6-7).

When Adam and Eve disobeyed God, they suffered a head-on collision with sin. They didn't die immediately upon impact but, as God predicted, the injuries would be terminal. They would not recover. Death was inevitable.

The first change to the man and his wife, after they sinned, regarded their eyes—the eyes of both were opened and they saw that they were naked. The initial brunt of the impact was sustained in their sexuality. Although virtually every area of their being was fractured, no aspect of their personhood was more directly and immediately traumatized. All their descendants up to the present have suffered the same wounding.

One way that brokenness surfaces is in the emotions we feel whenever the topic comes up. Just say sex and something flinches. The whole area of our sexuality is wounded, bruised, and sore to the touch. We feel various levels of embarrassment, shame, guilt, regret, condemnation, accusation, fear, anger, or remorse. Instinctively, we want to cover and hide our brokenness from God and others.

For those of us who truly love the Lord Jesus, we earnestly desire to please Him, especially in our sexuality. Many of us, however, feel like failures. For some, the fight for sexual purity is the foremost battle of our Christian lives, and one in which victories are too few. Tried, failed; tried, failed. We've read books, attended seminars, done small groups, had accountability partners, and yet the failures sometimes persist.

*The whole area of our sexuality is sore to the touch.*

What I'm about to claim is bold, but I'm persuaded that the vehicle for victory presented in this book has the potential to change things for you like no other tool you've ever employed. Why? Because it's officially sanctioned by the Holy Spirit, with ink, in God's word.

Let me begin by telling the story of my encounter with this powerful biblical tool.

## MY STORY

It was December of 2006. In the course of my daily Bible reading, I came to Job 31:1, "I have made a covenant with my eyes; why then should I look upon a young woman?" Total consecration to Jesus has always been my passionate pursuit, so I used this verse to prayerfully offer myself again to Him.

"Yes, Lord. Yes. I'm saying yes to You once more. I'm signing up for this all over again. My eyes are Yours. My heart is Yours. I'm fiercely resolved to walk in purity before You. I want to see You. Give me this verse."

I took several minutes to pray repeatedly in this manner when the Holy Spirit interrupted and gently whispered to my heart.

"You know you've never actually done it."

I was nailed.

Well, no Lord, I haven't actually made a *covenant* with my eyes. I mean, that's serious! That's like making a *vow* before You. Vows are scary! How could I ever make a covenant in the area of sexuality when it is characterized by so much brokenness and failure?"

But I was busted. I was saying yes to a verse without ever actually saying yes to it. I had made commitments and resolves but had never actually made a *covenant* with my eyes.

So I began to pray over the verse in earnest. "Lord, should I do this?" It grew increasingly clear to me that the Holy Spirit was extending an invitation. He was inviting me into greater consecration in my sexuality.

But I was terrified to make this kind of a vow. Why? Because I understood the seriousness of making a covenant with God. I'll explain more fully in chapter ten why an eye covenant is so terrifying, but one reason is because it provides no wiggle room for the flesh. A vow doesn't say, "Here's what I'll do if I blow it"; rather, it says, "I promise to never violate this vow, ever."

*I was saying yes to a verse without ever actually saying yes to it.*

That was petrifying!

That's why I took about a week to pray about it. I needed to discern exactly what the Spirit of God was offering me, and whether I had what it would take to follow through and adhere to the vow. I was counting the cost.

## I MADE THE VOW

It dawned on me that the fearful nature of the covenant was actually a gift. The whole point in making a covenant was to intentionally clothe myself in the terror of the Lord. The gravity of knowing I was in covenant with God would help me avert my eyes in a moment of temptation. I knew that if I was wise I would not shun this fear. "The fear of the LORD is the beginning of wisdom" (Psa. 111:10).

After a week of prayer, it became clear that a window of grace was open before me. God was inviting me to a covenant with my eyes, which meant He was offering the grace to keep it. With a trembling heart, I finally decided to do it. I wrote out my vow, entered it in my journal, dated it, and verbalized it in prayer to God.

It was one of the scariest days of my life.

Then I wanted to seal it with an offering (some vows in the Bible were accompanied by an offering or sacrifice to God, e.g. Num. 6:2), and I wanted the offering to be large enough that I would never forget this decision. I couldn't afford to make a vow like this and then forget about it in a moment of temptation. A large offering would help to make it memorable. After receiving my wife's permission, I dug into our savings and sealed the covenant with an offering to the Lord.

Learning to walk under the covenant at first was marked with some awkwardness and uncertainty. I thought of how it might have felt for David to learn warfare in a coat of armor he had never worn before (1 Sam. 17:39). This vow was a new coat for me, and I wasn't sure how to wear it.

I remember one incident, soon after making the covenant, when I was in a hotel room and thought I'd search for an educational channel. I held the TV remote in my hands, and had two fingers poised over the controls. I trembled as I checked out the channels, with my fingers ready to quickly change the channel if the wrong thing came on the screen. I actually held the remote with trembling hands—it was a first-time experience for me. I couldn't afford to stumble upon a channel that would compromise my covenant. I was learning my way with this new garment. How would I do life under this kind of vow? It took time for the new garment to feel comfortable on me.

## HOW A VOW HELPS US

The purpose of the vow is to seal our hearts for obedience in moments of vulnerability.

All of us have moments of vulnerability related to temptation. And most of us have an element of curiosity in our personality. When circumstances uniquely line up so that vulnerability happens to coincide with curiosity, we can end up in trouble rather quickly.

You may already know what I mean, but let me explain. Each of us has moments of vulnerability to temptation based upon how we tick as individuals. For some, it's when we're sad. For others, it's when we're happy. For some, it's when we're stressed. For others, it's when we're rejuvenated and feel relaxed. When you're in a place of emotional vulnerability, and then something comes along that piques your curiosity—it's a set-up for trouble. It's as though the planets align, and you're not even aware how susceptible you are to temptation in that moment.

That's where many of us get tripped up. Under normal circumstances, we would say no; but in a certain convergence of circumstances, we find ourselves doing something we normally wouldn't do. We begin to look. We keep the TV on the same program, or we click on the link, or we size up the person. We go there. And then the fantasies start. Curiosity, in a time of vulnerability, has bitten.

What we need is a covenant with our eyes—a promise in the presence of God that we'll never look upon it. The covenant forever removes the option of taking a curiosity check. You no longer have the liberty to stay with a program that you can tell is heading in a sensual direction. You no longer have the freedom to click on a questionable link. Your covenant takes the cross and plunges it through your curiosity.

The covenant has a preservative power. It will keep you, if you honor it. At a time when you might have otherwise been vulnerable and curious, the covenant rises before you, the fear of the Lord grips you, and your eyes turn away from compromise. This is its role—to preserve you in moments of weakness.

Since the day I made my eye covenant, I've been profoundly aware of its preserving hold. Its power has carried me. Its terror has gripped me.

What a gift!

## GREATER VICTORY AWAITS YOU

Here's my witness: From the day I made a covenant with my eyes, I instantly entered into a higher dimension of victory in the battle for sexual consecration. The difference was immediate and significant, and has endured to the present.

To clarify, I have not yet attained total victory over all temptation. The fight to overcome in our sexuality is never completely over until we're buried six feet underground. We all continue to fight in this war, progressing from strength to strength (Psa. 84:7). But I want to assure you of this: If the Lord leads you to make a covenant with your eyes, you'll enjoy new levels of victory in your walk. Expect the difference to be clear, palpable, measurable, and real.

Are you someone who wants to live in obedience to every part of God's word? If so, I challenge you to look again at Job 31:1, "I have made a covenant with my eyes." The Lord is calling you to unrestrained, wholehearted consecration in your sexuality. Is an eye covenant to be part of that consecration?

I waited for several years to write this book until I had personally proved the power of this covenant. Now that I have some history with God in this area, I declare with sincere conviction that this book may hold a critical key for your personal victory. Please track with me all the way to the end. If you'll stay with me, I'll articulate as clearly as I can one of the most glorious and powerful invitations available to you in the grace of God—a covenant with your eyes.

*Your covenant takes the cross and plunges it through your curiosity.*

This book isn't a comprehensive guide to every aspect of our sexuality. *It won't answer every question.* Rather, it's focused on one specific topic—a biblical tool designed by God to equip us for purity.

By the way, you will notice that I use *covenant* and *vow* interchangeably throughout this book—because the Bible does also.[1]

Realizing that this subject raises some questions, come with me now as I explain what a covenant is and why it's so helpful. I hope to answer most objections and provide practical advice for walking it out in the grace of God.

Let's begin by taking a closer look at the biblical concept of *covenant.*

## [ For Small Groups ]

**Dig:** Why did Job say he made a covenant with his eyes? What was going on in his life at the time? Study the verse's context.

**Share:** Tell the group why you joined this study. What are you hoping for, or asking of God, through this study?

**Pray:** Ask the Lord to speak to you as you read this book. Express your commitment to His will and your desire to grow in intimacy with Him.

1 The Hebrew for covenant is *bereeth* (Strong's 1285). The Hebrew for vow is *neder* (Strong's 5088). The Hebrew for oath is *awlaw* (Strong's 423) and *shebooaw* (Strong's 7621). The Hebrew for promise is *dawbawr* (Strong's 1697). While the meaning of each word is unique, there are times when their meanings overlap and become interchangeable, which is common among synonyms. You can see how these words are used interchangeably in the Old Testament by looking at how these Hebrew synonyms occur in Psalm 132:2 and Deuteronomy 23:23 and 29:14. *Promise* and *covenant* are interchangeable in the New Testament in Galatians 3:17 and Hebrews 9:15. As to their unique shades of meaning, covenants (*bereeth*) are usually with God and occasionally man; vows (*neder*) are always with God; oaths (*awlaw, shebooaw*) are equally with God and man.

# TWO

# The Strength of Covenant

*"I have made a covenant with my eyes; why then should I look upon a young woman?" (Job 31:1).*

To understand *covenant* as Job conceived it, it's helpful to realize that the book of Job is the oldest book in the Bible, put to writing centuries before Moses wrote Genesis. The idea of covenant has been around a long time. In sourcing this book we're tapping into some of the most ancient spirituality available to humanity.

Saints of the past often studied Job and Revelation together. That combination of the Bible's first and last books triggers a reminder of Jesus' words, "The last will be first, and the first last" (Mat. 20:16). Luminaries of past centuries recognized that the first mention of biblical truths often had particular significance for last days' believers. This interpretive principle suggests that the book of Job should be viewed as carrying an end-time message. How does this apply to Job 31:1? The verse becomes a prophetic declaration that, in the final days of this present age, a generation will excavate the patriarchal piety of the book of Job and make a covenant with their eyes.

The word *covenant*—as Job used it—is a strong word that puts you in a headlock and wrestles you to the ground. Job didn't simply make a commitment or a resolve; he made a covenant.

Its strength of imagery derives from the time God made a covenant with Abraham (Gen. 15:7-21). God told Abraham to cut three animals in half[1] and lay the pieces open on the ground, along with two birds. One implication of the cut pieces was that if the covenant was violated, the same destruction might fall on the violators as fell on the animals.

Then a smoking oven and burning torch—which represented God's person—passed between the pieces of flesh, and God repeated His fantastic promises to Abraham (Gen. 15:12-16). This was God's way of showing Abraham that His covenant with him was secure. Abraham was not asked to pass between the pieces. Passing through the pieces alone, God was indicating that He was committing Himself to the covenant regardless of how Abraham and his descendants might adhere to or violate it. God has never, and will never, relent from that covenant with Abraham.

This is how serious the idea of covenant was in those times. There was nothing glib or trite about it. So when Job said he made a *covenant* with his eyes, he was pulling out a sledgehammer word that rams into our chest.

Given the gravity of the biblical idea of covenant, please consider the following as a working definition for a covenant vow.

*Covenant is a sledgehammer word.*

A vow is a covenant that is solemnized by a verbal or written pledge and must never be violated—on pain of consequences.

## COVENANT ALWAYS INCLUDES GOD

Someone with a picayune penchant for semantics might look at Job's covenant and complain, "Job didn't make this covenant with God, he made it with his eyes. God wasn't involved."

But the word *covenant* implies God's involvement. When Job made this covenant with his eyes, he did so in the presence of God. His covenant meant, "God being my witness, I'll never allow my eyes to look upon a woman in a lustful way. My eyes won't do it. God helping me, it will not happen."

1 From this we get the term, "cutting a covenant."

To break the covenant with his eyes was to break covenant with God.

Solomon confirmed that covenant involved God when he spoke of a woman's marriage covenant as being "the covenant of her God" (Prov. 2:17). In other words, when a woman made a wedding covenant with her husband, she was also making a covenant with God. To break covenant with her husband was to break covenant with God. God's involvement in covenant was assumed.

A covenant with the eyes, therefore, is a three-way covenant: between your heart, your eyes, and your God.

## JOB'S STORY

The events leading to Job's vehement statement in 31:1 were quite astonishing.[2] God and Satan entered into a cosmic duel over Job, with Satan wagering that he could induce Job to curse God, and God claiming that Job would remain loyal to Him no matter what. With God's permission, Satan unleashed a torrent of adversity upon Job. He lost his income base and livelihood (all his flocks, camels, herds, and servants), he lost all ten of his children to a tornado, and then he lost his health (boils from head to toe). Even after all his losses, however, he refused to curse God (see Job 1-2).

*To break the covenant with his eyes was to break covenant with God.*

Then Job's three best friends came to comfort him. After sitting silently with him for seven days in dumbstruck grief, they began to engage in a philosophical debate concerning the cause of Job's plight. Their discourses, which comprise the majority of the book, are a brilliant and energetic dialogue on the causations of human suffering. The arguments of Job's friends can be summarized by this line of logic:

- God blesses the righteous and punishes the wicked.
- Job's adversity, therefore, must be punishment for great wickedness.

2 I commend to you the heartfelt book on Job I wrote, entitled, *Pain, Perplexity, and Promotion: a prophetic interpretation of the book of Job*. See oasishouse.com.

- Unless Job repents of his wickedness, he will not be released from divine judgment.

In contradiction to his friends, Job insisted that his calamities were not divine judgment on sin in his life. He maintained that he had lived a blameless, righteous life—and he held to his integrity throughout the entire dispute.

At the conclusion of the debate, Job substantiated his blamelessness by going into a detailed description of his righteous practices. He spoke of his integrity in business, marital fidelity, benevolence toward his servants, alms for the poor, his defense of the fatherless, absence of greed, abstention from idolatry, his hospitality, and the fair remuneration of his laborers. Chapter 31 is a roaring, deafening crescendo to a dialogue of epic proportions—the resounding testimony of a man in unimaginable pain who lifted his voice to the heavens and cried, "I have walked in integrity and uprightness before my God." At the top of his list was this compelling affirmation, "I have made a covenant with my eyes; why then should I look upon a young woman?" (Job 31:1).

Job was saying, "God can't possibly be punishing me for lustfully looking at other women. Years ago I made a covenant with my eyes, and I have honored it carefully. I vowed that I would not allow my eyes to look lustfully upon a woman. Ever since, I have reserved my eyes for my wife and my God."

I share this backdrop to convey the intensity of feeling with which Job spoke of his eye covenant. There was great passion and conviction in his voice. He was laying down a timeless standard for what constitutes a blameless lifestyle.

In case we might question Job's blamelessness, God Himself weighed in and testified to his uprightness. The way the story ends shows how God vindicates the righteous at the end of the day. It's a fantastic story, a must-read, a compelling testimony to the wisdom of making an eye covenant. We come away from the book realizing that God wasn't punishing Job for his sin but was using a most remarkable highlighter to underscore the power of purity.

## AN INVITATION, NOT A COMMAND

Notice that Job 31:1 isn't worded as a command. When the Holy Spirit inspired this for us, He didn't make it a directive for all believers. Rather, the narrative element in the verse gives it the tone of an invitation.

"Job did it—would you like to, too?"

To clarify, while Job's covenant isn't presented as a command, there *are* verses in the Bible that command us to be pure. For example, "Abstain from fleshly lusts which war against the soul" (1 Pet. 2:11). Or, "Put to death your members which are on the earth: fornication, uncleanness, passion, evil desire, and covetousness, which is idolatry" (Col. 3:5). Without question, we're commanded to be pure. What isn't commanded is the *means* we use to attain that goal. Each believer has the freedom to discover the means that is most helpful to him or her.

A covenant with the eyes is a means to purity. It's a tool. It's a divinely sanctioned, practical, empowering tool to help us walk in consecration. We aren't commanded to make this covenant, but its wisdom is certainly advanced in Job 31.

The sense of the invitation is this: "If you're especially eager to gain victory over fleshly lusts and please the Lord in your sexuality, you're invited to make a covenant with your eyes. It's the most violent and effective way to neutralize compromise where it usually starts—at the eye gate."

*A covenant with the eyes is a means to purity. It's a tool.*

To see what I mean by "the eye gate," let's now turn to the next chapter because it all centers around the eyes.

## [ For Small Groups ]

**Dig:** Study the covenant God made with Abraham in Genesis 15, and bring your observations to the group. Can you improve on the definition for covenant supplied in this chapter?

**Share:** Talk about tools God has given us to remain pure before Him. How many come to mind? Is it helpful to see a covenant with our eyes as a tool?

**Pray:** Pray over Colossians 3:5 together. Ask the Lord to increase our eagerness and ability to obey this verse.

## THREE

# The Eye Gate

*Turn back the battle at the gate (Isa. 28:6).*

The great battle today is for your eyes. Heaven and hell are in an epic struggle to gain your gaze. Why?

*Because the eye is the gate to our sexuality.*

Picture a castle, with a gate that regulates all incoming and outgoing traffic. Whatever the eye permits determines the nature of the traffic in the heart.

To engage in the battle for sexual purity, we must start with our eyes. Until the eye gate is subdued and surrendered to the Lordship of Jesus Christ, the high ground of purity cannot be held.

Actually, the eye is a gate to more than just our sexuality. It opens to many areas of desire, including things like food, drink, possessions, etc. I'm sure John had all areas of desire in mind when he wrote about "the lust of the eyes" (1 Jn. 2:16), but in this book I am focusing specifically on the way the eye triggers our sexuality.

> *The eye is the gate to our sexuality.*

The eye is not the *only* gate to our sexuality. Later I will mention ears, hands, and nose—hearing, touch, and smell—which are secondary gates. They are a *distant* second, however. Except for the visually impaired, the eye is the primary gate, and once it is subdued, the others easily come into subjection. The eye is the first and great gate to be mastered.

## THE BIBLE CONNECTS EYES WITH SEXUALITY

The connection between eyes and sex is readily affirmed in Scripture. For starters, we can mention again the leading text for this book, "I have made a covenant with my eyes; why then should I look upon a young woman?" (Job 31:1). But that's not the only Bible verse to link the two.

When the Bible speaks of the sexual desire Potiphar's wife had for Joseph, it connects it to her eyes. "And it came to pass after these things that his master's wife cast longing eyes on Joseph, and she said, 'Lie with me'" (Gen. 39:7).

Solomon addressed the eye/sex link when he warned his son about the harlot's snare. "Do not lust after her beauty in your heart, nor let her allure you with her eyelids" (Prov. 6:25). The word *lust* refers to a sexual desire that is sinful. If not careful, a young man's eyes can be snagged by a harlot's beauty, and then her eyes pull him in for the kill.

Jesus Himself drew a clear connection between eyes and sexuality.

> But I say to you that whoever looks at a woman to lust for her has already committed adultery with her in his heart. If your right eye causes you to sin, pluck it out and cast it from you; for it is more profitable for you that one of your members perish, than for your whole body to be cast into hell (Matt. 5:28-29).

Peter also acknowledged this connection when he described false leaders in the church as, "having eyes full of adultery and that cannot cease from sin, enticing unstable souls" (2 Pet. 2:14). These leaders were using their influence among the people to entice unstable believers to sin. Their hearts were full of adultery, and you could see the lust seething inside by following their eyes. The gate of their eyes was wide open to immorality.

It's a rare instance when sexual temptation has absolutely no connection to the eyes. Almost every sexual temptation that hits you is somehow channeled through this gate.

Theaters, TVs, computers, mobile devices, tabloids, and people are powerful conveyors of temptation. This is why provocative programs zoom in on the eyes of the actors and actresses. They're looking at her, she's looking at them; he's looking at her, she catches his eye. Eyes full of adultery lock with eyes full of adultery. And the viewers, entering vicariously into the scene, become eyes.

It's all about the eyes.

## THE BATTLE AT THE GATE

As the gate to our sexuality, the eyes are the first things assaulted in our battle with temptation. I use the word *battle* because James 4:1 describes the fight for purity as an all-out war. What we allow or forbid at our eye gate determines the conditions under which we fight for sexual consecration. Let me explain.

If your eye gate is sealed shut, the enemy is kept outside your castle (your life) and you can fight him from a position of strength. If the gate is relaxed and sometimes found open, temptation will gain access to the inside of your castle—into your mind and heart—and now you are very vulnerable. You're still trying to put up a fight, but you can't gain the upper hand because the enemy has slipped inside the gates of your castle.

*What we allow or forbid at our eye gate determines the conditions under which we fight for sexual consecration.*

When I compare our lives to a castle, I'm employing the imagery of cities during Bible times. Large stone walls were erected around a city, making it a veritable fortress so it could withstand attack from foreigners. Gates were made of iron. When under attack, the city gates would be drawn shut, and the city's warriors would take their positions on the wall to repel invaders.

Invading forces always targeted the gate first. Since the city walls were usually very thick, the gate was the most vulnerable part of the fortress's structure. Battering rams always went after the gates. If the attackers could just penetrate the gate and get inside, the city would quickly fall. This is why Isaiah 28:6 spoke of "those who turn back the battle at the gate." The defenders inside the city would take their stand on the wall and fight to defend the city gates from being breached.

Picture that city under siege. That's a snapshot of your fight for sexual purity. Temptation wants to penetrate and set up camp inside your mind. You're under incessant attack, and if you can keep the enemy on the outside of your castle, you can remain victorious in your fight for consecration.

But if your eye gate is compromised, you're toast.

## THE EYE FEEDS THE MIND

If the eye is the gate to the castle, the mind or heart is the inner courtyard. (The mind and heart are often interchangeable terms biblically. See Genesis 6:5, for example, where it speaks of "the thoughts of the heart.") When it comes to sex, your mind is the control tower or main hard drive. Jesus confirmed this when he portrayed the heart as the ground and center of all sexual activity (Mat. 15:19).

The eye triggers the mind—that is, whatever the eye allows determines the atmospheric conditions of the mind. When the eye rests upon something and sends its data to the mind, the mind takes and runs with it.

If the eye is good, it will forbid entrance to tempting images and only grant access to light and truth, filling the whole body with light (Mat. 6:22). If the eye is bad, it will allow darkness to penetrate the heart until the heart is bound in darkness and even the body is full of darkness (Mat. 6:23).

James described how temptation works when it's allowed access to our castle (Jam. 1:14-15). If allowed to enter, it awakens sinful desires in the heart. The mind grabs it, dwells on it, and the desire grows. Eventually that desire conceives and gives birth to sin. Sin, once full-grown, eventually ends in death. Gaining control of the eye gate, therefore, is a matter of life and death. What you allow through your gate can literally kill you.

What a mighty little gate!

To change metaphors for a moment, lust is a forest fire in the heart. The fire is fed on three fronts: the eyes (sight), the ears (hearing), and the hands (touch). To master the forest fire, you must engage the fire on all three fronts. For example, if you're not looking at sensual images but you're listening to sensual music, the fire won't abate. All three senses of sight, hearing, and touch must be addressed. But start with the eyes. Once you firmly close the eye gate, victory in the other areas will come much more swiftly.

*What you allow through your eye gate can literally kill you.*

How do we shut the eye gate? By making a covenant with our eyes.

An eye covenant doesn't eradicate or silence temptation; it keeps it outside our lives. It denies stimulating visuals from gaining access to our minds because we absolutely refuse to look in temptation's direction. A closed eye gate lifts us to the high ground of mastery over temptation. We're high on the wall, thwarting every attempt of the enemy below, and contending for a pure thought life from a place of advantage.

If you already have complete victory in your sexuality, then you don't need this book. But if you find that, despite your best resolves to walk in purity, you have moments of vulnerability to temptation, the message of this book may be especially helpful for you. If it seems there's sometimes a tiny crack in the door of your heart, and you open to certain kinds of compromise, an eye covenant has the power to take that crack and seal it shut.

## THIS IS A NARROW GATE

It's not easy to make a covenant with your eyes. You'll probably encounter various emotions, such as, "It's scary to make this kind of a covenant with God—what if I blow it?" Or, "Am I really ready to never again feast my eyes?" It's like forever kissing good-bye the sinful indulgences that have consoled and fed your flesh.

This vow is a death to self. It's a crucifixion. It hurts. It kills.

We feel a sense of loss. The flesh wants to know, "You mean, I'll never again be allowed to have another look?" Answer: No.

The command is clear. "Therefore put to death your members which are on the earth: fornication, uncleanness, passion, evil desire, and covetousness, which is idolatry" (Col. 3:5). That area in your members doesn't want to die. It will clamor for even a tiny air hole. To obey Jesus, you must utterly suffocate it. Then drive a sword through it. The most practical and helpful way to put to death your members, as it relates to sexual sin, is to make a covenant with your eyes.

Jesus said, "Narrow is the gate and difficult is the way which leads to life, and there are few who find it" (Mat. 7:14). Putting your members to death is narrow and difficult. But here's the wonder of it: Once you do it, you enter into the joy of Spirit-empowered obedience where you're freed from the bondage of sin. It's like a grace-awakening in which you discover that the "narrow" and "difficult" (Mat. 7:14) is actually "easy" and "light" (Mat. 11:30).

## THE FINAL FRONTIER

Once the eye gate has been mastered and sealed shut, the traffic in our souls calms down, and we can progress to the final frontier in our quest for consecration: the heart. Scripture reveals that the heart, which is the true essence of a person, is the central and ultimate battleground of this struggle:

> But I say to you that whoever looks at a woman to lust for her has already committed adultery with her in his heart (Matt 5:28).
>
> The heart is deceitful above all things, and desperately wicked; who can know it? (Jer. 17:9).
>
> For as he thinks in his heart, so is he (Prov. 23:7).
>
> Keep your heart with all diligence, for out of it spring the issues of life (Prov. 4:23).

First we close the eye gate through an eye covenant; then we go for the jugular—our thought life. This is the realm of fantasy, imagination, aspiration, and desire. If our thought life is pure, our sexuality will be expressed in purity and honor; if our thought life is impure, it will eventually find expression in sinful actions.

Scripture instructs us to exercise control over our thoughts: "bringing every thought into captivity to the obedience of Christ" (2 Cor. 10:5). An eye covenant doesn't "fix" your thought life; it only prevents new visual data from gaining entrance. But all the old data and thought patterns are still swirling in the heart, even after you make a covenant with your eyes. So make the covenant—and then tackle your thought life.

An eye covenant equips you to tackle this great and final frontier. If you are to walk in consecration, it is *essential* that you enter aggressively into the battle for your thoughts. Every thought must be made to bow to Christ, one at a time. If you make a covenant with your eyes, but continue to allow fantasies to run wild in your heart, the waters of your heart will never become clean and clear.

Don't make a covenant with your mind. Don't say, "I vow to never think an impure thought." That kind of vow would set you up for failure. Who has the ability to never again think an impure thought? Make a covenant with your eyes, not your mind.

As regards your eyes, make a covenant; as regards your mind, make resolves. Resolve in your heart to bring your thoughts into submission to Christ. Let your resolve be, "As the Lord grants His grace, I'm going to do warfare against every impure thought until each one is submitted to the Lordship of Christ."

We have the mind of Christ (1 Cor. 2:16), which means we have the ability, by the power of the Spirit, to gain mastery over impure thoughts. It is inexcusable, in Christ, to allow fantasies to trample our hearts unchecked. Hunker down. Fight for your heart. Every time an impure thought fills your heart, deal ruthlessly with it by taking it to the cross. Replace it with thoughts that are noble, just, pure, lovely, and virtuous (Phil. 4:8). Prepare yourself to fight, even to your last breath, for a pure heart. The Holy Spirit is ready and waiting to help you in this good fight of faith (1 Tim. 6:12), and your eye covenant will enable you to fight it well.

## THE POWER OF AN EYE COVENANT

An eye covenant carries remarkable ramifications for every area of your sexuality. Make it, and you'll be amazed at its ripple effects—that is, at how many other issues it engages and addresses. Here's just a few examples.

- It will determine what programs you watch and what songs you listen to.
- It will govern what you allow yourself to read.
- It will alter how you look at men and women.
- It will change how you speak conversationally with others.
- It will impact your computer usage.
- It will affect the things you buy.
- It will guide how you touch others.

What a powerful tool the Lord gave us when He equipped us with Job's covenant. It cuts to the chase and seals off the gate.

### [ For Small Groups ]

**Dig:** What connection do you see between the eyes and the heart? How does the eye trigger the heart? What verses can you find that show the connection?

**Share:** Was it helpful to view the eye as the gate to our sexuality? Why? Was it helpful to see the heart as the final frontier?

**Pray:** Is there any way you feel the enemy has gained access to the inside of your castle through the eye gate? Pray for one another.

PART TWO

# Appreciating the Covenant

You will appreciate the wisdom of an eye covenant when you see how effectively it helps us gain victory over temptation.

FOUR

# A Weapon for Our Times

*For the weapons of our warfare are not carnal but mighty in God for pulling down strongholds (2 Cor. 10:4).*

At first glance, a covenant with your eyes might seem a little extreme or excessive. But when you consider the intensity of today's battle, it's not overkill. It's the most wise and reasonable response to such an intense assault from hell. It's a weapon for our times.

I'll state the obvious: We're in a war! Sexual images accost us at every turn—enticing, luring, tempting, seducing. You don't have to be a rocket scientist to see it; it's everywhere. We're hit when we go to school, when we go to work, when we use the computer, when we watch TV, when we go to the grocery store, and even when we drive down the road. Can the barrage be escaped?

Like never before, compromise is accessible, affordable, and anonymous. One click on the device in your hand can deliver it to you immediately. Sometimes it seems as though an entire generation is being swept up in a tsunami of sin that is disqualifying them from their divine destiny.

*Compromise is accessible, affordable and anonymous.*

Without question, hell has launched an offensive against today's generation to take down their purity and incarcerate them in lifestyles of immorality. I don't need to cite any shocking statistics to convince you—you know it's bad and getting worse. Casualties are everywhere.

But why today? Why now? Why the unprecedented assault?

## AN EPIC END-TIME BATTLE

It has to do with how natural history will end. To understand the nature of the warfare, all we need do is look at the last book of the Bible, the book of Revelation.

> Then I looked, and behold, a Lamb standing on Mount Zion, and with Him one hundred and forty-four thousand, having His Father's name written on their foreheads...These are the ones who were not defiled with women, for they are virgins. These are the ones who follow the Lamb wherever He goes. These were redeemed from among men, being firstfruits to God and to the Lamb. And in their mouth was found no deceit, for they are without fault before the throne of God (Rev. 14:1, 4-5).

This passage describes a company of one hundred and forty-four thousand at the very end of natural history, just before Jesus returns, who are of the tribes of Israel (Rev. 7:4-8) and who are "not defiled with women, for they are virgins." Their most striking characteristic is their radical commitment to sexual consecration. Just when the barrage of sexual filth is at its apex, there will be a generation living in unprecedented purity and devotion to Christ.

Satan doesn't want this generation of consecrated virgins to arise in the earth because:

> *Just when the barrage of sexual filth is at its apex, there will be a generation living in unprecedented purity and devotion to Christ.*

- As "firstfruits to God," they will be the first among many—that is, they will be anointed to call multitudes to the same consecration they model. The impact of their ministry will derive from their purity. Gentiles around the world will follow their lead and remain undefiled.
- Encouraged and strengthened by

the ministry of the two witnesses of Revelation 11:3-13, these virgins will be anointed and released to minister in great authority in the Holy Spirit, preparing the planet for the imminent return of Christ. Satan's kingdom will suffer some of its greatest setbacks because of their ministry.

- Their faithfulness, therefore, will contribute to the events that precipitate the return of Jesus Christ to earth (2 Pet. 3:12), Satan being bound in prison for a thousand years (Rev. 20:1-3), and then ultimately Satan cast into the lake of fire (Rev. 20:10).

Satan knows that the spiritual authority on the ministry of this last days' company will be predicated upon the purity of their consecration, so he's using his full strength to tempt today's generation with sexual compromise. If he can successfully keep God's people bound by compromise, the return of Christ will be delayed indefinitely, and the judgment God has reserved for him will be thwarted. The war is on!

I have a question about these undefiled ones of Revelation 14. With so much temptation on every side, how will this end-time company keep themselves pure and remain virgins? Will they keep themselves because they're passionately in love with Jesus? Past generations have had that, but it wasn't enough. Will they keep themselves because they're deeply committed to sexual purity? Past generations have had that, but it wasn't enough. It will require more than commitment or resolve. It will require covenant.

There's only one way they will keep themselves as virgins in the hour of sin's greatest profusion: by *making a covenant with their eyes*. It's the only way. Only the grace that is released through this kind of abandonment will keep them undefiled. The wisdom of spiritual violence will manifest. They will make vows with God and be fiercely devoted to keeping them.

## VIRGINITY RESTORED

Someone might wonder, "But I've already fallen to sexual sin; does that mean I'm eternally disqualified from being one of these virgins and serving in Christ's army?" Not if you're willing to repent, renounce the ways of sin, and consecrate yourself to purity. Here's where Christ's blood arrests us with its power to cleanse. "If we confess our sins, He is faithful and just to forgive us our sins and to cleanse us from all unrighteousness" (1 John 1:9). Paul said that if we will cleanse ourselves of dishonorable iniquities, we will be "a vessel for honor, sanctified and useful for the Master, prepared for every good work" (2 Tim. 2:21).

I'm persuaded Jesus can restore the most sin-ridden heart to the purity of virginity. Here's why I believe that.

In Psalm 45:14, the bride of Christ is portrayed on her wedding day as approaching King Jesus, and it says, "She shall be brought to the King in robes of many colors." In Bible times, virgins wore robes of many colors as a symbol of their virginity (2 Sam. 13:18-19). The "robes of many colors" the bride will wear as she comes to the King indicates that she's a virgin in His eyes. In other words, at the marriage supper of the Lamb, the bride of Christ won't be presented to Jesus as a used, defiled harlot with a long history of spiritual adultery; rather, she'll be presented to King Jesus as a virgin, "not having spot or wrinkle or any such thing, but that she should be holy and without blemish" (Eph. 5:27). How is it that we, who have whored after the world, can be presented on that day to Christ as a chaste virgin? Surely this is a glorious tribute to the efficacy of the shed blood of Calvary, which is so powerful it can restore us to the pristine purity of virginity!

*Jesus can restore the most sin-ridden heart to the purity of virginity.*

Repent, let the blood of Jesus restore you to virgin purity, make a covenant with your eyes, and become a participant in raising up a Revelation 14 generation of undefiled virgins. God has a plan to raise up a devoted end-time generation that will surpass their predecessors in consecration and spiritual exploits. You can be a spiritual father or mother to this generation.

The only way you'll be able to call a generation to make a

covenant with their eyes is if you yourself have also made one.

## KNOW YOUR ENEMY

*The only way you'll be able to call a generation to make a covenant with their eyes is if you yourself have also made one.*

In this kind of epic warfare, it's important that you identify who your true enemy actually is. So let me present it as a question.

What would you say is the Christian's foremost enemy? Would you say it's Satan? The world? Or the flesh? Actually, enemy number one is *sin*. Sin is your primary enemy because it has the power to kill you.

Your ultimate enemy is death, but sin is your primary enemy right now because it's the thing that leads to death, as seen in these verses:

> Therefore, just as through one man sin entered the world, and death through sin, and thus death spread to all men, because all sinned (Rom. 5:12).
>
> The wages of sin is death (Rom. 6:23).
>
> Sin, when it is full-grown, brings forth death (Jam. 1:15).

Get it: Sin is your biggest enemy—because it leads to death. It can kill your relationship with God, and it can kill your eternal destiny.

Satan is highly aware of sin's power. That's why he tempts you. His primary strategy isn't to stab you through with a pitchfork; his primary strategy is to lure you into sin. When you're sinning, he's happy. He knows that sin has power, all by itself, to drag you to destruction. And he knows it brings you under God's judgment (Eph. 5:5-6). Satan wants God relating to you in an adversarial way. He wants you to pick a fight with God.

Know your enemy. Satan isn't your first enemy, sin is. Sin can do more harm to you than all of hell's forces combined. Satan deceives you but sin kills you.

Declare war on sin! Do whatever it takes to triumph over sin and temptation. Use every weapon available to you:

repentance, confession of sin, the cleansing of Christ's blood, prayer, the truth of God's word, faith, accountability to others, the power of the Holy Spirit, dying to self, etc.

*Satan deceives you but sin kills you.*

But in addition to all these powerful weapons, add an eye covenant to your arsenal. Why? It's one of the most violent, aggressive measures available to you to overcome sin.

## VIOLENT TIMES REQUIRE VIOLENT MEASURES

Today's fight for purity is unprecedented, but certainly not new. This battle has been fought from the beginning of time. Looking back to the era of Israel's judges, the tribes of Israel *literally* went to war to fight for sexual purity. The tribe of Benjamin defied the other eleven tribes because they defended the right of their relatives to practice homosexuality and gang rape. It ended in a God-endorsed battle that nearly wiped out the entire tribe of Benjamin (please read Judges 19-20). The war for purity is *ancient*. What's new today is the battle's *intensity*.

We shouldn't be surprised that the war's intensity is growing. After all, the Bible predicted today's immoral bombardment (Rev. 9:20-21; 2 Tim. 3:1-4; 2 Pet. 3:3; Jude 1:17-18). We must counter, however, in a fitting manner. Higher levels of attack demand higher levels of response.

We can't answer today's attacks with yesterday's weapons. What helped yesterday's generation won't suffice today. The rules have changed. Just as technology has changed the face of modern warfare (you don't fight drones with hand grenades), the nature of today's sex wars demands new strategies. Let me explain.

The counsel given to yesterday's generation, when placed in the context of today's blazing techno-battle, comes up anemic, insipid, and impotent. Consider the advice I collected from one source, which represents the counsel yesterday's generation received:

- You can't stop women from passing within eyeshot, but you don't need to take it any further.
- Stop looking intently, and the temptation will quickly go away.
- There are women who enjoy dressing provocatively. Accept and deal with it.
- If you're to overcome this temptation, it'll be up to you.

These kinds of "helpful hints" aren't going to preserve someone who is caught in the vortex of today's fiery temptations. It's like trying to fight a forest fire with a water pistol. We're in the fight of our lives. Pastors are being derailed; young people are being enslaved. We've stepped into an epic, cosmic clash of titanic forces. We need more than tips and suggestions—we need solutions with grit, with substance, with teeth.

In this kind of a war zone, we need fierce wartime strategies that grab the kidneys. We need spiritual violence. When I say *spiritual violence*, I have Jesus' words in view, "And from the days of John the Baptist until now the kingdom of heaven suffers violence, and the violent take it by force" (Mat. 11:12).

*We need solutions with grit, with substance, with teeth.*

What kind of spiritual violence do we need? An eye covenant! The intensity of today's fight demands it. Knowing the deadly capacity of sin, this covenant suddenly comes into focus for its brilliant wisdom. As a tool that empowers obedience, it can literally preserve your life.

## [ For Small Groups ]

**Dig:** Find and list the verses in Revelation that seem to best describe the war we're in today.

**Share:** In what ways have you seen the battle for sexual purity increase in recent years? Do you think an eye covenant is one of God's answers for the intensity of today's fight?

**Pray:** Using Matthew 11:12, pray for each person in your group to be a strong warrior for Christ in this hour. Ask the Holy Spirit for help.

## FIVE

# One All-Inclusive Vow

*Flee sexual immorality (1 Cor. 6:18).*

One reason an eye covenant is so wise and powerful is because, if it is carefully honored, it will safeguard your heart from almost every kind of sinful sexual practice. Most sexual temptations come to the eye gate first, and if we covenant to never let our eyes look upon such things, most sexual sins will be stopped before they have a chance to start. Or in baseball language, sexual sin won't even get on first base.

To show what I mean, first of all let's identify sexual sin. Living in a day when some Christian teachers are influenced by the cultural values of the world and redefining what God considers to be sinful, it's necessary to clarify exactly what constitutes sexual sin.

## WHAT SEXUAL BEHAVIOR IS SINFUL?

Sexual sin, as shown by God's word, is all sexual activity outside the covenant of conjugal marriage. (Conjugal marriage is marriage between one man and one woman.[1]) "Marriage is honorable among all, and the bed undefiled; but fornicators and adulterers God will judge" (Heb. 13:4).

1 The Bible does not explain why God allowed polygamy in the patriarchal era, although the allowance was certainly an expression of His mercy. Over time, God increasingly revealed His will that men marry just one wife. See Ephesians 5:31-33 and 1 Timothy 3:2, 12.

So-called "gay marriage" isn't honored by God because He only joins a man and woman in marriage. As Jesus said, "So then, they are no longer two but one flesh. Therefore what God has joined together, let not man separate" (Mat. 19:6); God performs no such joining for same-sex couples.

Several Bible passages list behaviors that God considers sinful (Lev. 18:6-30; 20:10-21; Eph. 5:3; Rom. 1:26-32; Mat. 15:18-19; 1 Cor. 6:9-10). For the sake of brevity, here are just two passages.

> Now the works of the flesh are evident, which are: adultery, fornication, uncleanness, lewdness, idolatry, sorcery, hatred, contentions, jealousies, outbursts of wrath, selfish ambitions, dissensions, heresies, envy, murders, drunkenness, revelries, and the like; of which I tell you beforehand, just as I also told you in time past, that those who practice such things will not inherit the kingdom of God (Gal. 5:19-21).

> For this reason God gave them up to vile passions. For even their women exchanged the natural use for what is against nature. Likewise also the men, leaving the natural use of the woman, burned in their lust for one another, men with men committing what is shameful, and receiving in themselves the penalty of their error which was due (Rom. 1:26-27).

Fornication often refers to sexual activity among unmarried people. The Bible sometimes uses it as a general term for all sinful sexual behavior. The desire of every sincere believer is to shun all sins that displease the Lord because of our fidelity to Him.

## YOUR VOW WILL KEEP YOU FROM ADULTERY AND FORNICATION

*Sexual sin is all sexual activity outside the covenant of marriage.*

If you honor your eye covenant, you will never participate in adultery or fornication. Why? Because those sins involve the eyes. Adultery automatically has you looking upon another person in a sexual way. If you honor your vow to never look at someone else in that manner, then you won't even flirt with or touch that other person. Your eye covenant won't allow it. Your vow allows you to be involved sexually only with your spouse.

The Bible doesn't tell us if Joseph had a covenant with his eyes. But it does tell us that when Potiphar's wife made her moves on him, he ran from her presence (Gen. 39:7-12). When you have an eye covenant, but then someone tries to seduce you to commit fornication or adultery, your only option is to *run*! You can't stick around to take a second glance.

The Bible doesn't tell us if David had a covenant with his eyes. If he did, he violated it when he looked on Bathsheba. If David had made a covenant with his eyes and honored it, he would have turned away when he got that first look at Bathsheba bathing. Instead, he indulged his eyes, and it led to adultery.

Keep an eye covenant and adultery will never happen.

The same holds true for other sexual sins such as homosexuality, lesbianism, orgies, bestiality, rape, incest, molestation, human trafficking, etc. If you vow before God to never let your eyes look upon any who might participate in these kinds of sins, you'll keep yourself in purity before God.

Now I want to show how an eye covenant will help you with two sins that are very common today: pornography, and masturbation.

## YOUR VOW WILL KEEP YOU FROM PORNOGRAPHY

*Keep an eye covenant and adultery will never happen.*

When you make a covenant with your eyes, you vow to God to never look lustfully upon a man or woman—whether in person, or in an image. It's impossible to honor an eye covenant and view pornography or sexually stimulating images.

Some people suppose pornography is okay because it's not specifically mentioned in the Bible. It's true that it's not mentioned, but the Bible does address it in principle. For starters, the Greek word *porneia*, from which we get our English word *pornography*, does appear in the New Testament. It's the Greek word for *fornication*. *Porneia* is defined as illicit sexual intercourse and can include adultery (Mat. 5:32; 19:9).[2] The way the New Testament uses *porneia* makes it a broad term for all sinful sexual activity, so in that broad sense it can include the viewing of pornography.

When viewing pornography, you are looking at a man or woman to lust after them. When you lust after another person, Jesus said you are committing adultery in your heart. His comments in the following passage clearly include looking at pornography.

> You have heard that it was said to those of old, "You shall not commit adultery." But I say to you that whoever looks at a woman to lust for her has already committed adultery with her in his heart. If your right eye causes you to sin, pluck it out and cast it from you; for it is more profitable for you that one of your members perish, than for your whole body to be cast into hell (Mat. 5:27-29).

Jesus plainly taught that anything which produces lust in the heart is producing sin. Without question, therefore, pornography is sin. It's not physical adultery; but, as Jesus said, it's adultery in the heart.

> Viewing pornography is adultery in the heart.

When Jesus spoke of plucking out your right eye, He was showing how aggressive and violent we must be in eradicating sin from our hearts and lives. He meant that if plucking out your eye is what it would take for you to get victory over looking lustfully on women or men (which is what pornography is all about), better to be without an eye for a few years than to burn in hell forever.

Some married couples try to convince themselves it's okay to view pornography in their bedroom because they're using it within their marriage covenant. Your bed might be undefiled because your sexual partner is your spouse (Heb. 13:4), but your spirit is darkened and defiled because your heart is committing adultery.

2 *Vine's Expository Dictionary of New Testament Words*, p. 455.

Pornography has no place in the life of the believer. Ever. It makes no difference whether it's straight sex, gay sex, pedophilia, bestiality, or some other form of sex. *All* forms of porn are sinful.

For those struggling with same-sex attraction, pornography is enemy number one. Do violence to it! Make a covenant with your eyes.

The temptation to view pornography is very strong for some people. This is why an eye covenant is such a brilliant gift from heaven. When we vow with our eyes to never look on it, the tempting images are denied access to our hearts through our eye gate. With the temptation now on the outside of our lives, we are able to gain traction in our pursuit of holiness and purity.

In overcoming pornography, an eye covenant is nothing short of *fantastic*!

## USE YOUR VOW TO FIGHT MASTURBATION

An eye covenant will help you *tremendously* in your fight to overcome masturbation. I will explain how in a moment, but first I want to explain why masturbation is something to be resisted and overcome.

I need to show why masturbation is sinful because some Christian teachers, in a compassionate attempt to help those who struggle, have construed ways to make it okay before God. I also am very compassionate toward those who struggle, so I want to address it gently and kindly. However, I also want to represent God's word faithfully.

When practiced as a means of self-release in isolation, masturbation is wrong because of the lust that accompanies it.[3] Bottom line, the issue is lust. Called by some "solo sex," it's committing adultery in the heart because it involves lusting for a man or a woman. Jesus' words on this deserve to be quoted again.

3 One exception might be when supplying a sperm sample to a doctor for medical reasons, while guarding the heart.

> You have heard that it was said to those of old, "You shall not commit adultery." But I say to you that whoever looks at a woman to lust for her has already committed adultery with her in his heart. If your right eye causes you to sin, pluck it out and cast it from you; for it is more profitable for you that one of your members perish, than for your whole body to be cast into hell. If your right hand causes you to sin, cut it off and cast it from you; it is more profitable for you that one of your members perish, than for your whole body to be cast into hell (Mat. 5:27-30).

Notice that when Jesus spoke of adultery in the heart, He also spoke about "your right eye" and "your right hand." Although He didn't name pornography and masturbation, He addressed the heart issues involved, at least as practiced by men. For men, the "right eye" of pornography operates in tandem with the "right hand" of masturbation, producing adultery in the heart.

If cutting off your right hand is the way you'll stop committing adultery in your heart (masturbation being one way that can happen), Jesus was saying it's better to be without a hand for a few years than to burn in hell forever.

Jesus was not actually advocating physical dismemberment here, which is seen from His use of the word, "If." Everyone knows that gouging out the right eye will not remove the desire to look at lustful images with the left, and cutting off the right hand will not remove the desire to masturbate with the other. The fundamental problem is not that the eye wants to look or that the hand wants to masturbate; the problem is with the heart. In saying "cut it off," Jesus' point was, deal violently with sin in the heart. An eye covenant is one way to resist sin violently.

*Deal violently with sin in the heart.*

In addition to Jesus' words, I will cite three other Bible passages that help us discern the heart of God on the issue of masturbation.

> But fornication and all uncleanness or covetousness, let it not even be named among you, as is fitting for saints (Eph. 5:3).

"All uncleanness": Paul made this a category of sexual sin. Uncleanness would refer to any sexual sin that defiles the spirit, soul, or body. Instead of naming masturbation, Paul names the larger category. Masturbation is a defiling sin that comes under the category of uncleanness. It is defiling because of the lust that attends it. Those committed to forsaking all uncleanness will forsake masturbation.

Furthermore, Paul wrote:

> Flee also youthful lusts; but pursue righteousness, faith, love, peace with those who call on the Lord out of a pure heart (2 Tim. 2:22).

What did Paul mean by "youthful lusts"? He was talking about lusts that teens participate in when their bodies are changing and they are discovering things about their sexuality. That process of self-discovery sometimes involves sinful experimentation. Masturbation is just one of those "youthful lusts." Why would I call masturbation a youthful lust? For two reasons. First, masturbation often starts when people are in their youth—in their teen years and discovering how their sexuality works. Second, it is often a stronger temptation for teens than for those who are old enough to be married and can express their sexuality properly through marital intimacy. In warning about youthful lusts, Paul meant more than *just* masturbation, but masturbation was included in the lusts he intended. If you agree with my interpretation, then we should take this verse to mean that we should flee masturbation.

And here's a final verse from Paul that is relevant to this topic.

> The wife does not have authority over her own body, but the husband does. And likewise the husband does not have authority over his own body, but the wife does (1 Cor. 7:4).

One thing Paul meant is that a wife doesn't have authority over her own orgasm, but her husband does. And likewise a husband doesn't have authority over his own orgasm, but his wife does. Your orgasm is the sole right of your spouse. You don't have the right to give yourself a sexual release. When you do, you infringe upon your spouse's authority and violate this Scripture. If you'll obey this Scripture, pornography and masturbation will never be able to displace the God-ordained intimacy of the marriage bed.

This verse also speaks to singles. If you're unmarried, you don't have authority over your own orgasm. Only your future spouse has that right.

Based on these verses, masturbation doesn't belong in the life of a believer. Those who are fiercely committed to obeying the verses just quoted will conclude that masturbation must go.

Sometimes single Christians, in wanting a release from sexual desire, have asked if it's okay to masturbate if it's done without engaging in any lustful fantasies. But I consider the possibility of doing so too unrealistic to be considered a valid option. For the single believer who desires to please Jesus in their sexuality, the best way to live in victory over lustful thoughts is to remain sexually inactive (no masturbation). While it might seem to give some temporary relief from sexual desires, it raises one's general sense of sexual "aliveness" or consciousness, which militates against a single believer's quest for consecration.

> You don't have the right to give yourself a sexual release.

If you're in agreement that masturbation is something to be resisted and overcome, I have good news for you: An eye covenant is the single most powerful tool available to help you in this fight.

God was so wise in giving us the eye covenant. When we sincerely take the vow and honor it, we'll never allow our eyes to rest or dwell upon images or people that stimulate lustful thoughts. If our eyes unexpectedly see something tempting, we immediately honor our vow and avert our eyes. How does this help us overcome masturbation? By cutting off the images to the mind that arouse lustful thoughts.

When the flow of new stimulating traffic to the mind is stopped, we staunch the fuel line that has been supplying our fantasy life. Now we can fight, by the power of the Holy Spirit, to still the old traffic we have accumulated in our minds. The grace of Jesus helps us wrestle down fantasies and engage in the glorious task of "bringing every thought into captivity to the obedience of Christ" (2 Cor. 10:5). As we do so, the impulses that pressure us to masturbate grow quieter.

Once lustful thoughts have been subdued and replaced with thoughts that honor Christ, masturbation loses its power. As you are filled with the power and fruit of the Spirit (Gal. 5:23), self-control will enable you to climb to the summit and obtain overcoming victory.[4]

If you want to be a disciple of Christ and deal violently with sexual sin, the violence of an eye covenant is perfectly designed for you. Yes, the vow is extreme. It's radical. It's violent. And it's just what we need. It equips us powerfully to overcome virtually every kind of sexual sin, through the enabling grace of Christ.

### [ For Small Groups ]

**Dig:** In your studies, which do you think is the strongest verse in the Bible calling us to sexual purity?

**Share:** Do you agree that pornography and masturbation are wrong? Why or why not? What seems to be the consensus the Holy Spirit is giving our group? Would you want to share how you've overcome?

**Pray:** Is there a certain sin that you would like to confess, if it is group-appropriate to do so? Pray for one another in accordance with James 5:17.

4 If you want additional help with overcoming masturbation, do your own internet search and also check out the resources mentioned in the Appendix, page 143.

## SIX

# Saved From Great Transgression

*"Therefore the one who delivered Me to you has the greater sin" (John 19:11).*

Another reason an eye covenant is so wise and advisable is because it can keep you from heading into great transgression. Let me explain.

A progression of sin seems to be indicated in the following verses:

> Who can understand his errors? Cleanse me from secret faults. Keep back Your servant also from presumptuous sins; let them not have dominion over me. Then I shall be blameless, and I shall be innocent of great transgression (Ps. 19:12-13).

The progression of sin is shown in the words, "...errors...secret faults...presumptuous sins...great transgression." It all can start with something as tiny as a small error. When little errors are unconfessed and allowed to germinate, however, they can lead to secret faults; secret faults grow into presumptuous sins; and finally, presumptuous sins can lead to great transgression. Great transgression is dreadful—because it incurs great judgment.

The message of the passage seems to be that sin grows. It escalates. Sexual sin rarely remains static. Often it progresses toward increasing levels of darkness.

Ephesians 4:22 points to this when it says, "the old man

which *grows corrupt* according to the deceitful lusts." Lust is deceitful because it has a way of growing increasingly corrupt. What starts off small can grow and tumble, until it becomes an habitual sin that renders us slaves to sin (John 8:34). The tentacles of sin just keep wrapping around your body and soul until you're dragged to destruction.

Make a covenant with your eyes and arrest the progressive nature of sin. When you make an eye covenant and then adhere to it through the enabling grace of Jesus, the power of habitual sexual sin in your life will be broken.

One of the harmful lies circulating in the body of Christ is the notion that no particular sin is worse than any other. The purpose of this lie is to deceive people who are bound in great darkness to think lightly of their sin. Satan doesn't want them to know how destructive their sinful behavior actually is to them.

Jesus Himself said that some sins are greater than others (John 19:11, above). In the Bible, greater sins incur greater punishments (Deut. 17:8; Mat. 26:24; Heb. 10:29; 2 Ki. 23:26; 24:3). If all sins are equally wrong, then it would be unjust to assign different levels of punishment for different sins.[1]

*An eye covenant can deal a death blow to the curse of habitual sin.*

An eye covenant, properly employed, will save you from the judgment of great transgression. To explain my meaning, let's look at a few examples of the greater sexual sins.

## SINNING AGAINST OTHER PEOPLE

Some sexual sins involve sinning against another person. When you sin all by yourself, that's bad. But when you sin against someone else, you can come under the judgment of great transgression. An eye covenant can save you from that kind of judgment by keeping you from sexual sins that involve others. Let's look at some examples.

1 Jack Hayford explains why sexual sins are often worse than other kinds of sins in his short book, *Fatal Attractions: why sex sins are worse than others.*

An eye covenant will keep you, as we said in the last chapter, from fornication—which involves sinning against another person. It will also keep you from adultery, which is a sin both against the other person and the spouses involved. Paul warned us that these kinds of sins against other people incur God's judgment.

> For this is the will of God, your sanctification: that you should abstain from sexual immorality; that each of you should know how to possess his own vessel in sanctification and honor, not in passion of lust, like the Gentiles who do not know God; *that no one should take advantage of and defraud his brother in this matter, because the Lord is the avenger of all such*, as we also forewarned you and testified. For God did not call us to uncleanness, but in holiness. Therefore he who rejects this does not reject man, but God, who has also given us His Holy Spirit (1 Thess. 4:3-8).

When Paul said, "that no one should take advantage of and defraud his brother in this matter," the word *defraud* means:

- to make a gain at the expense of another.
- to cheat somebody out of something.
- to take more from another than what is right.

The passage warns, "the Lord is the avenger of all such." In Revelation 2:20-23, we have an example of how Jesus avenges sexual immorality: with sickness, great tribulation, and death. Make no mistake, there are some sins that God judges more severely.

An eye covenant is so wise! It will keep you from defrauding other people.

But there are even greater transgressions that an eye covenant will save you from. Not only will it preserve you from consensual sins like adultery, it will also keep you from non-consensual sexual sins like molestation, incest, abuse, and rape. God sees all such instances of violation, He sees how the victims are traumatized and scarred, and He *will* bring these transgressions to account.

Jesus spoke directly to sins that offend other people, especially sins committed against the "little ones":

> Then He said to the disciples, "It is impossible that no offenses should come, but woe to him through whom they do come! It would be better for him if a millstone were hung around his neck, and he were thrown into the sea, than that he should offend one of these little ones" (Luke 17:1-2).

I can't imagine the horror of standing before Jesus on Judgment Day and having a sin like abuse, incest, or rape on one's record. Much better to be drowned in the sea!

It's possible that you may want to make an eye covenant, but think, "I've already blown it. I've already violated someone in this way. Is it too late for an eye covenant? What do I do now?"

*If you've ever sinned against someone through rape or molestation, get it off your record.*

If you've ever sinned against someone else through rape, incest, or molestation, I advise you to do whatever you must to get it off your record in heaven. I realize that in cases of rape or molestation, our sin against another person may also constitute an illegal crime, which complicates the situation. However, if getting a sin off our record in heaven means that it is brought into a human court because we confessed it, it is still better to make it right before God. If your record is not yet clear in heaven, do not allow the fear of disclosure's consequences to keep you from making it right.

The following three principles speak to instances where we have been the perpetrators of rape, incest, or molestation. Seek pastoral counsel, ask the Holy Spirit to speak to you regarding these Scriptures, and then obey the Lord.

- Principle #1: Confess it to God. "If we confess our sins, He is faithful and just to forgive us our sins and to cleanse us from all unrighteousness" (1 John 1:9).
- Principle #2: Confess it to an objective, mature believer, and ask them to pray for you. "Confess your trespasses

to one another, and pray for one another, that you may be healed" (Jam. 5:16). Realize that if a crime has been committed, that person may be legally obligated to report your crime.

- Principle #3: Be reconciled, if possible, to the person against whom you have sinned. "Therefore if you bring your gift to the altar, and there remember that your brother has something against you, leave your gift there before the altar, and go your way. First be reconciled to your brother, and then come and offer your gift" (Mat. 5:23-24).

Don't go to your brother if your brother has nothing against you. But if your brother has something against you, you have a command from Christ to obey.

In cases of abuse and molestation, receive competent pastoral and legal counsel before approaching someone you've violated. One reason to receive pastoral counsel first is to be sure that your confession is expressed in a way that promotes healing and reconciliation rather than additional hurt. Shallow confessions such as, "I'm sorry if I hurt you," or, "I never meant to harm you," are prideful and hurtful. Don't minimize your sin, but own it in its worst terms—for example, if it was rape, call it rape. Confess in complete contrition, "I sinned against you. I violated and hurt you. It was totally my fault. I am so sorry. Please forgive me. I want us to be reconciled according to Matthew 5:24."

Get unresolved sin taken care of *before* Judgment Day. But do it in a way that promotes healing, not further hurt. Call on the Lord to help and guide you by His Spirit. Then make an eye covenant that you determine to honor for the rest of your days.

Great transgressions are troubling and need to be cleansed, forgiven, and resolved. But even better—make a covenant with your eyes and don't allow these sins any entrance whatsoever to your eye gate.

## SINNING AGAINST YOUR OWN BODY

An eye covenant will also preserve you from sinning

against your own body. Here's what Paul said about that.

> Flee sexual immorality. Every sin that a man does is outside the body, but he who commits sexual immorality sins against his own body (1 Cor. 6:18).

The Greek construction of "Every sin" is emphatic, meaning, "Every sin whatsoever." Paul was saying that sexual immorality is a greater transgression than many other sins because it's also a sin against one's own body. Some sins defile only a part of your being, such as your mind or your spirit, but sexual sins defile your entire person—spirit, soul, and body.

"What's so bad about sinning against your own body?" someone might wonder.

You're the steward and protector of your body. Your duty is to keep your body filled with light through meditation in the word (Luke 11:34), and to keep it holy as the temple of the Holy Spirit (1 Cor. 6:19). Nobody else will do this for you. When you sin against your own body, you grieve the Holy Spirit (Eph. 4:30), and violate your duty as your body's protector. With your body defiled and darkened, now you're vulnerable to even more sin. With every unrepentant failure, your body gets darker on the inside and increasingly vulnerable to sin. This is the cyclical pattern of sin that eventually leads to death (Jam. 1:15).

*In our battle with sin, our body can either help or hinder us.*

In our battle with sin, our body can either help or hinder us. Jesus pointed to this when He said:

> The lamp of the body is the eye. Therefore, when your eye is good, your whole body also is full of light. But when your eye is bad, your body also is full of darkness. Therefore take heed that the light which is in you is not darkness. If then your whole body is full of light, having no part dark, the whole body will be full of light, as when the bright shining of a lamp gives you light (Luke 11:34-36).

When your body is full of light, it becomes a vehicle to actually aid in your pursuit of righteousness. But if your body is full of darkness, it pulls your soul and spirit into darkness as well.

You want your body to be an ally, not a detriment—so make your eye good! Make a covenant with your eyes, and fix your eyes firmly upon Christ and His word. Get your body filled with light. It will be a fantastic asset as you serve God.

## GODLY OFFSPRING

When you read the Bible, you see how strongly God is opposed to sexual sin. Why is it such a big deal to Him?

The primary reason is given in Malachi 2:15.

> But did He not make them one, having a remnant of the Spirit? And why one? *He seeks godly offspring*. Therefore take heed to your spirit, and let none deal treacherously with the wife of his youth.

God wants sex reserved for marriage because He's eagerly seeking godly children. God gave us marriage, in His wisdom, because it's the optimal context to produce godly children. Every kind of sexual sin hazards the sanctity and safety of marriage.

Marriage is the foundation of the family unit, and God is intensely opposed to anything that weakens or destroys it. Why? Because He wants godly offspring.

This is why Romans 1:26-27 portrays homosexuality and lesbianism as greater transgressions than fornication or adultery. When all moral standards that constrain sexual behavior are removed, and homosexuality becomes acceptable and normative, rather than raising godly offspring, a generation will raise defiled offspring.

*Every kind of sexual sin hazards the sanctity and safety of marriage.*

God's search for godly offspring is at the very heart of the entire topic of human sexuality. Anything that hinders the raising up of godly offspring is a serious sin in the sight of God.

This is why an eye covenant is such a wise and glorious gift to us. It will keep us from great transgression, and will direct our hearts toward our spouse and children so that we might raise up godly offspring in the earth.

An eye covenant—what a brilliant gift!

### [ For Small Groups ]

**Dig:** Read Malachi 2, to see verse 15 in its context. How does Malachi 2 speak to you in your pursuit of consecration?

**Share:** Talk about how an eye covenant can keep us from sinning against others. What are wise and proper ways to resolve sins that we've committed against other people in the past?

**Pray:** Let's ask the Lord to forgive us for ways we've sinned against others. Ask Him to show us the wisest and most redemptive way to be reconciled to anyone that might have something against us.

PART THREE

# Trembling Under the Covenant

An eye covenant activates the terror of the Lord, which will stop you short in moments of temptation.

# SEVEN

# Gas Pedal, Brake Pedal

*Turn away my eyes from looking at worthless things,*
*and revive me in Your way (Psa. 119:37).*

The previous section showed the compelling wisdom of making an eye covenant.

- It provides a violent tool sufficient for today's violent war (chapter four).
- It nips virtually all forms of sexual sin in the bud by dealing with it where it tries to start—at the eye gate (chapter five).
- It has the potential to save us from the judgment of great transgression (chapter six).

Most books that address sexual sin, in seeking to deter us from incurring God's judgment, use the approach of the previous chapter—they motivate us toward purity by highlighting the negative consequences of sin. Those consequences are real and true. However, when the flames of temptation are swirling around your mind and the fiery darts of the evil one are striking your passions, fear of sin's consequences isn't always enough to keep you.

Maybe you've experienced what I mean. You know how horrible the sin is—and you know how it's eating your peers alive—but you still stumble stupidly into the same pit. As you're yielding to temptation, you're thinking to yourself, "This is wrong, this is wrong, this is wrong," but it's not enough to stop you—you just keep sliding into the mire.

If the fear of sin isn't enough to keep us from compromise, what will it take? What will actually secure our hearts and keep us from falling in the hour of temptation?

Complete victory over sexual temptation will be found when two things are burning within our hearts like a blazing inferno:

- the love of Christ, and
- the fear of the Lord.

Now we're getting down to the nitty-gritty of this book.

Picture your life as a car. To direct your life into victory and steer clear of ditches, you must have two things operational in the car of your life: a gas pedal and a brake pedal. A gas pedal moves you forward in the right direction, and a brake pedal stops you from going in the wrong direction.

The gas pedal is the love of Christ; the brake pedal is the fear of the Lord.

## GAS PEDAL

First, let's talk about the gas pedal. In the pursuit of purity, the gas pedal is our passion for Jesus that propels us forward into wholehearted obedience. We love Him so much that our hearts long to obey and please Him. And little wonder—He gave His last gasping breath and spilled His last drop of blood in order to bring us into His family. We now inherit, together with Christ, the massive wealth of our heavenly Father. We owe Jesus *everything*! Now we yearn to please Him with every waking moment.

*The gas pedal is the love of Christ; the brake pedal is the fear of the Lord.*

We want this love to grow and abound more and more! We want to feed the fire of this love. Just as He loves us with all His heart, all His soul, all His mind, and all His strength, we desire to love Him with all our heart, all our soul, all our mind, and all our strength. We can't love Him, in the strength of our flesh, as He deserves; we need His help. It takes God to love God (1 John 4:19). This is why God pours His love into our hearts by the Holy Spirit (Rom. 5:5)—so that His love might empower us to reciprocate and love Him in the same way He loves us.

Love—it's all about love! The last thing love wants to do is disobey or disappoint Him. We're lovesick! We want everything that hinders love to be swept away, and we want everything that strengthens it to be fanned aflame.

Put the pedal to the metal! Press into this love of Christ. Set your heart to pursue affectionate obedience. As you push aside every hindering sin and pursue the limitless love of Christ, your heart will come alive to the extravagant affections of your gracious heavenly Father.

Jesus said, "He who has My commandments and keeps them, it is he who loves Me" (John 14:21), and here's what He meant. When you use the gas pedal of love to press forward into greater obedience, Jesus takes it personally as an expression of your loyalty to Him.

When you make a covenant with your eyes, you're saying, "Jesus, You're everything that I want to see. I turn my eyes from every worldly affection and set them upon You. I devote myself to loving You and talking to You from Your word. Abba Father, give me the spirit of revelation in the knowledge of Christ, that I might come to know Him better" (see Eph. 1:17-19). The Holy Spirit will answer your prayer by steering your life into the love of Christ and the will of God.

If you want to walk in purity, the first and greatest key is to abandon your heart in love to Christ. Like a gas pedal, love will catapult you forward into an abiding relationship with Jesus. It will empower your secret place and fuel your intimacy with Jesus.[1] As you devote yourself to prayer and Scripture

1 To strengthen your pursuit of Christ in the word and prayer, I urge you to see my book, *Secrets of the Secret Place*. This book is being used significantly by the Lord to equip believers to grow in the knowledge of God. It will help stoke the fires of your intimate love relationship with Jesus. See christianbook.com or amazon.com or oasishouse.com.

meditation, the Holy Spirit will enable you to fulfill the first and great commandment (Mat. 22:38). This gas pedal of love is fantastic! It will accelerate you forward into obedience, sanctification, purity, and faith.

## DRAW THE WALLS CLOSER

Love doesn't ask, "How far can I go in lust before I lose His presence?" Rather, love wants to know, "How far from lust will God's grace empower me to walk?"

Imagine a furnace or wood stove. If you push out the walls of a stove, the fire grows cold. If you pull the walls in close, the fire grows hot. Suppose the furnace represents your romance with Jesus, and the walls of the furnace represent the standards of purity you erect around your life. The same dynamic with the walls holds true. If you loosen the standards of what you allow by pushing out the walls, the fire disperses and your love for Jesus grows cold; but if you rein in your distracting "freedoms" by pulling in the walls of what you allow, the embers cluster and your love for Jesus grows more fiery.

Love wants to draw the walls of consecration in close, to make the flame brilliant and pure. Sin hinders your ability to receive God's love, but obedience fans the flame.

When you're walking in sexual purity your eyes are clear, your spirit is bright, your body is full of light, your heart is alive and responsive to God, and the river of affectionate exchange with Jesus flows freely. It's *the* way to live!

> *Pull in the walls of what you allow, and your love for Jesus will grow more fiery.*

I'm talking about love as a gas pedal that propels us into the face of Christ. I'll get to the brake pedal in a moment, but I have a couple more things to say about the gas pedal.

## WE WANT TO SEE GOD

I'll tell you the leading reason why I made a covenant with my eyes: I want to see God. This desire is the driving motivation of my life. I want an audience with the King. Psalm 84 says that the saint who is on the high road of spiritual pilgrimage ultimately "appears before God in Zion" (Psa. 84:7). Destination God. No hope is dearer to me.

Jesus said it with thundering clarity, "Blessed are the pure in heart, for they shall see God" (Mat. 5:8). This is why I pursue consecration so fervently. This is why I've made a covenant with my eyes—I want to see God. Like Job did.

Here's the stunning thing about Job's journey. The man who made a covenant with his eyes was the man who one day beheld God face to face. While still in the body. The Bible intends for us to make that connection between his eye covenant and his seeing God. God rewarded his purity of heart. When he saw God he said, "I have heard of You by the hearing of the ear, but now my eye sees You" (Job 42:5).

One day my lips will utter those words, "Now my eye sees You." I don't know when. It may not be until the next life. But my hope is that I won't have to wait that long. My hope is that I might see Him in this life, just like Job did. And Abraham. And Moses. And Joshua. And Ezekiel. And Daniel. And John. Jesus affirmed that there are some who get to see God in His glory in this lifetime (Mat. 16:28), and my heart wonders earnestly if I might be in that company. This much I know: If I'm to see God, I must devote myself to purity of heart.

*The man who made a covenant with his eyes was the man who one day beheld God face to face.*

No compromise is worth forfeiting this hope. Anything that might diminish the hope of beholding the glory of the Lord is my dread enemy.

Jesus said that purity gets the greatest of all possessions: God Himself. I have no higher aspiration. He alone is my portion and exceedingly great reward. No price is too costly for this great acquisition, this Pearl.

God is the greatest delight of the human soul. God, who is the author of pleasure, knows how to bring pleasure to the human spirit at much higher and nobler levels than sin ever could. The pleasures of sin are a cheap counterfeit. Why would I sacrifice the superior pleasures of knowing and loving God for temporary pleasures that dull my spirit and rob me of His favor?

That settles it. I'm making a covenant with my eyes—I want to see God!

## JOSEPH'S STORY

I want to touch on Joseph's story again because it's so instructive to our study. When Joseph was taken to Egypt, he became the slave of a man named Potiphar. Potiphar so trusted Joseph that he made him steward over all his household affairs. Later, while fulfilling his duties in the house, Joseph was approached by Potiphar's wife who tried to seduce him (Gen. 39:7-12). In response, he ran from her.

I marvel at Joseph. He was a young man with natural hormones, he was far removed from family, and he had a chance with a beautiful woman. Nobody would ever need to know. I've often wondered, what kept him from committing adultery with Potiphar's wife?

The answer is found in the things Jacob had imparted to Joseph in his youth. Jacob had taught him about God's remarkable promises to his great-grandfather, Abraham (Gen. 15:12-21). Jacob probably said things like, "Joseph, you're next in line. If you'll walk in integrity and obedience to God, you can inherit the blessing God promised your great-grandfather." What Joseph caught from his father was a passion for his spiritual inheritance. Joseph probably knew that Reuben had lost the inheritance by committing adultery with one of his father's wives (Gen. 35:22; 49:4). Determined to receive what Reuben had forfeited, he said no to Potiphar's wife because he valued his spiritual inheritance.

Joseph knew he couldn't burn with her fire and also burn with God's fire. He had to choose which fire he wanted. Bottom line, Joseph wanted God more than he wanted the girl.

*Joseph knew he couldn't burn with her fire and also burn with God's fire.*

You can't see Potiphar's wife and see

God. You must decide what you want to see.

Is your desire to see God a blazing fire that propels you, like a gas pedal, into obedience to Christ?

## BOTH GAS AND BRAKE

I've been likening love to a gas pedal that propels us forward into the heart of Christ. But to drive a car successfully, you need two pedals: a gas pedal and a brake pedal. The brake represents the fear of the Lord. We must have both love (gas) and fear (brake) if we're to get to our destination safe and sound.

If you have a passionate love for Christ (a peppy gas pedal) but don't have a functioning brake system in the fear of the Lord, you're eventually going to crash. To walk in purity you must have both the love of Christ and the fear of the Lord operating effectively in your life.

Said succinctly, the love of Christ propels you into purity, and the fear of the Lord stops you from crashing into compromise.

This twofold motivation is laid out plainly by Paul:

> Knowing, therefore, the terror of the Lord, we persuade men... For the love of Christ compels us (2 Cor. 5:11,14).

Paul said two things motivated him to labor in the harvest. He was motivated by the terror of the Lord because he understood the horrors of eternal damnation; and he was compelled by the love of Christ because he knew how much Christ loves people. Both motivations, when combined, formed a complete incentive for abandonment to the harvest.

We need those same two inducements if we're to move forward in holiness and purity. We need the love of Christ to spur us forward into that which promotes holiness, and we need the fear of the Lord to stop us short of anything defiling.

Love and terror. It's the twofold strategy for consecration.

## COMING UNDER THE TERROR OF THE LORD

*The love of Christ propels you into purity, and the fear of the Lord stops you from crashing into compromise.*

Love for Christ is the first and great impetus for sexual consecration. However, love by itself isn't enough to keep us pure. That's a bold statement, so let me support it with a Scripture.

When Jesus spoke to the believers in Thyatira, He commended them for their love, but in the next verse He rebuked them for their sexual immorality.

> "I know your…love…Nevertheless I have a few things against you, because you allow that woman Jezebel, who calls herself a prophetess, to teach and seduce My servants to commit sexual immorality and eat things sacrificed to idols" (Rev. 2:19-20).

Jesus affirmed that they truly did love Him, but their passion for Him was not enough to keep them from sexual immorality. What did they lack? The fear of the Lord. Deceptive teachers hadn't properly taught them in the fear of the Lord. As a result, their brakes weren't working.

Sometimes you need good, hard-grabbing brakes. Sometimes you need to stop. When you're moving in a wrong direction, if you just keep on moving forward with that other person, you'll both crash together. You need a brake. You need the terror of the Lord to be a blazing inferno in your soul so that when you hit the brakes, they actually work.

The common wisdom in the body of Christ suggests that the brake to keep you from crashing into compromise is the fear of sin's consequences. So they take a lot of time to tell you about the horrible things sin will do to you. Those consequences are true and we need to know them—as already stated—but the knowledge of sin's consequences is a poor braking system, demonstrated by the crashes of many who knew them. Others say that you should make yourself accountable to others, and the fear of knowing you'll have to report to your accountability partner will stop you. I'm a proponent of accountability, but again, that's not always

*Sometimes you need to stop.*

enough to stop you in the heat of temptation. You need something with bite, with grab. There's only one fear that is strong enough to deter you every time in a moment of weakness and temptation, and that is the utter terror of the Lord.

How do we come under the terror of the Lord? By making a covenant before God with our eyes. We actually say to God, "I vow to never let my eyes rest upon it."

Many times you can't prevent your eyes from seeing an image for the first time. Often it's beyond your control—boom—suddenly it's there. But you can prevent your eyes from taking a second drink. The eye covenant is a refusal to entertain that image. You don't violate the vow if your eyes catch something unexpectedly; you violate the vow if you choose to let your eyes dwell upon it.

If we're to walk in purity in today's sex-saturated society, we must engage a twofold strategy: We must pursue the superior pleasures of loving and being loved by God; and we must come under the terror of the Lord by making a covenant with our eyes.

Gas and brake. This is the twofold strategy that must sweep the earth in this hour.

I want to explain how an eye covenant brings us under the terror of the Lord, which is the primary purpose of this book. However, before we get to that, I need to answer some questions about making vows with God.

## [ For Small Groups ]

**Dig:** How can we grow in the love of Christ? Collect a few Scriptures that show the way.

**Share:** Let's talk about how the fear of the Lord is the brake that keeps us from crashing. How is the fear of the Lord different from "the fear of consequences"?

**Pray:** Tell the group how you want to grow in the love of Christ and the terror of the Lord. Then express your prayer to God.

EIGHT

# Is it Still Biblical to Make Vows?

When we talk about making covenants or vows with God, some leaders in the body of Christ have strong reservations. Realizing that this topic is controversial, my purpose in this chapter is to answer the most common objections to the making of covenants.

## "VOWS ARE OLD TESTAMENT, NOT NEW TESTAMENT"

Our leading text for this book (Job 31:1) is in the Old Testament, and most of the Scriptures dealing with vows and covenants are in the Old Testament, so one objection to vows is that they're an Old Testament reality not a New Testament practice. It's claimed that the cross of Christ abrogated the invoking of vows, making them no longer useful or applicable to New Testament believers.

In actuality, however, vows were practiced on two occasions in the New Testament church. The first time was in Acts 18:18, where it says that Paul "had taken a vow." Later, we're told of four believers in Jerusalem who had also taken a vow (Acts 21:23). The Holy Spirit gave us two witnesses to vows in the New Testament, thus satisfying the criteria of 2 Corinthians 13:1, "By the mouth of two or three witnesses every word shall be established." With two examples of New Testament vows, it's difficult to claim that they're abrogated by the cross.

There's a third New Testament mention of vows that's

indirect and harder to see, but it's there for those who are willing to recognize it. In Matthew 19:12, Jesus affirmed the integrity of eunuchs "who have made themselves eunuchs for the kingdom of heaven's sake." When Jesus spoke of eunuchs making themselves eunuchs, He wasn't speaking of self-mutilation; He was meaning that some believers will voluntarily take a vow of celibacy in order to be more devoted to the kingdom of God. Thus, Jesus was extolling the beauty and honor of making a vow of sexual consecration.

In addition to these three New Testament witnesses, Isaiah spoke of a time, after the cross, in which Egyptians will make a vow to God.

> Then the LORD will be known to Egypt, and the Egyptians will know the LORD in that day, and will make sacrifice and offering; yes, they will make a vow to the LORD and perform it (Isa. 19:21).

It seems that Isaiah had the millennial kingdom in view. Whatever the timing of its fulfillment, it's clear that this Scripture has not yet been fulfilled. There's coming a day when Egyptians will both vow to the Lord and perform it. If Egyptians will make vows in that day, it's safe to say that making vows to the Lord is still a biblical practice today.

I have one final argument to support the idea that vows are still fitting in today's New Covenant era, and this argument regards marriage vows. Someone might ask, "But where in the Bible does it say that marriages were sealed with a covenant?" In two passages, actually. In the first, Solomon described the immoral woman as someone "who forsakes the companion of her youth, and forgets the covenant of her God" (Prov. 2:17). Solomon affirmed that, at weddings, couples make a covenant both with each other and with God.

In the second passage, the Lord rebuked men who were divorcing their wives by saying, "Yet she is your companion and your wife by covenant" (Mal. 2:14). God Himself acknowledged that marriages were solemnized by covenant. We see that it's biblical, therefore, to exchange vows at wedding ceremonies.

If the cross had rendered vows unbiblical, then marriage vows would be wrong. But I think we all agree that it's still holy and noble for a couple to vow themselves to one another on their wedding day.

Our conclusion, therefore, is that vows are still valid in this New Testament age.

The next objection is even stronger.

### "JESUS FORBADE THE TAKING OF VOWS"

There are some who believe it's wrong to take vows today because they say Jesus prohibited them. The words of Christ they have in view are also referenced by James in his epistle. Here are the two passages they have in mind:

> Again you have heard that it was said to those of old, "You shall not swear falsely, but shall perform your oaths to the Lord." But I say to you, do not swear at all: neither by heaven, for it is God's throne; nor by the earth, for it is His footstool; nor by Jerusalem, for it is the city of the great King. Nor shall you swear by your head, because you cannot make one hair white or black. But let your "Yes" be "Yes," and your "No," "No." For whatever is more than these is from the evil one (Mat. 5:33-37).

> But above all, my brethren, do not swear, either by heaven or by earth or with any other oath. But let your "Yes" be "Yes," and your "No," "No," lest you fall into judgment (Jam. 5:12).

Are these passages forbidding vows? Actually, no. Virtually all commentators agree that in speaking against the swearing of oaths, Jesus wasn't addressing vows. Here's what Jesus was after.

In those days, to convince someone of your honesty, it was common practice to swear an oath that you were telling the truth. Over time, the practice took on tricky subtleties and nuances. For example, if you swore by the name of God, your oath was considered binding (because to break it meant you took the Lord's name in vain); but if you swore by something lesser than God, such as the temple, then

*If the cross had rendered vows unbiblical, then marriage vows would be wrong.*

you could get out of the oath by trivializing it, "Well, you know, I never did actually swear by God Himself. So I didn't take the Lord's name in vain." They developed all kinds of complicated rules to make it okay to get out of an oath.

Jesus decreed that when you swear by heaven, it's as binding as using the name of God.

Instead of saying, "I swear by heaven that I'm telling you the truth," Jesus told them to simply say "Yes" or "No." "Yes, that's the truth." "Yes, I will do that." "No, I didn't do that." When they got into subtle twists on words, they were actually co-operating with the evil one. The devil was in the semantics.

Jesus was saying, "Your word is your word. There's no such thing as a non-binding oath. So don't swear by anything. Just be true to your word. If you say yes, then it's yes. Or if you say no, then it's no."

The two above passages don't address vows to God at all; they address the swearing of oaths between people.

Peter fell into the trap of swearing oaths at Jesus' crucifixion. "Then he began to curse and swear, 'I do not know this Man of whom you speak!'" (Mark 14:71). When Peter cursed, he wasn't uttering profanities or expletives; he was calling down curses upon himself if he was not telling the truth. And when he swore, he was swearing by heaven, or by Jerusalem, or by God, or some other important entity. It was excessive practices like Peter's that caused Jesus to forbid these oaths.

Swearing of oaths to people was forbidden by Christ; vows to God were not forbidden.

Someone might argue, "Jesus never took any vows, so I'm not going to either. I'm only going to do what Jesus did."

In response, I would like to present evidence that it's possible Jesus did, in fact, make vows to God. We see this possibility in Psalm 22, which is a messianic psalm about the cross and the sufferings of Christ. In this psalm, the Messiah is quoted by David as saying, "My praise shall be of You in the great assembly; I will pay My vows before those who fear Him" (Psa. 22:25).

> *It's possible Jesus did, in fact, make vows to God.*

David was prophesying that the Messiah would both make vows and pay them.

What were Jesus' vows? We aren't told, but I'll offer my best guess. I think it's possible, when He was in Gethsemane and looking ahead to the cross, that He may have prayed along the lines of, "Abba, if You'll deliver Me from death and Sheol and raise Me up again to Your right hand, then I vow to..." And of course we can only imagine what kind of action Jesus might have vowed to the Father. This would come under the category of a conditional vow. "Father, if You'll do such-and-such, then I'll do such-and-such."

One day you may watch as He pays those vows.

Since Jesus didn't forbid the taking of vows, but actually seems to have made vows to God Himself during His time on earth, our conclusion is that vows are still legitimate for us today.

The next objection is perhaps the strongest of all.

## "VOWS ARE A VEHICLE OF CONDEMNATION, NOT GRACE"

In my opinion, the strongest argument against making vows to God is right here. The argument goes something like this:

"If a person makes a covenant with their eyes and then violates that covenant, they are likely to come under intense levels of accusation and condemnation. Anything that produces condemnation in the life of a believer is of the accuser. 'There is therefore now no condemnation to those who are in Christ Jesus, who do not walk according to the flesh, but according to the Spirit' (Rom. 8:1). Anything that is a vehicle for condemnation is outside the grace of God."

Those holding to this argument would counsel believers to make resolves rather than vows. They would rather that believers resolve themselves, in God's grace, to walk in purity, and if they violate their resolve, they can return to the Lord for forgiveness, get back up, and begin a fresh start. They see resolve as a vehicle of grace and a vow as a vehicle of condemnation.

The concern here, which I share deeply, is that believers not foolishly set themselves up for condemnation by taking a vow prematurely or inadvisedly. Imagine, for example, someone expressing themselves like this: "I've been resolved to walk in sexual purity for a long time, but I keep on experiencing failure. I struggle regularly with intense levels of condemnation, guilt, and accusation because of the failures. Sometimes I hardly know how to live with the guilt of failing in my resolve. If I make a covenant with my eyes and then have a failure at *that* level, I can't *imagine* the weight of guilt and despair I would encounter. I think it could bury me. Why would I want to increase my commitment from a resolve to a covenant, when at the resolve level I'm already under a huge load of guilt and accusation?"

I care deeply about this objection and will give it my best answer.

If a vow is invoked prematurely, it can in fact become a vehicle of greater condemnation. This is why I emphasize in this book that it's very important to make a vow in the right timing. You need to have a firm conviction in the Holy Spirit that you're ready to make a vow, and that the grace of God is inviting you into it.

First of all, I agree with my objectors that trying to fulfill a premature vow in the strength of the flesh is a recipe for catastrophe. When believers get in a performance mode and try to overcome sin through will-power, they're headed for inevitable failure—because no one is capable of overcoming sin in the power of the flesh. The last thing we want is for believers to become saddled with accusation because of a premature vow.

This is why I hesitated for years to speak about this covenant—because I didn't want to burden people with a yoke of bondage. But then I began to think about the alternative. If you don't make an eye covenant, but give yourself the leeway to have the occasional indulgence with

*When believers try to overcome sin through will-power, they're headed for inevitable failure.*

sin, sin is the *worst* kind of bondage. Staying at the resolve level saves you from violating a vow, but it also keeps a crack open in the door to temptation. An eye covenant slams the door shut, thus giving you the best opportunity to overcome bondage.

If an eye covenant seals shut a doorway of sin, it's not a source of bondage but of freedom. Closing the door fully is the only wise option for freedom from sin.

There's a way to make a covenant with your eyes that isn't contrary to, but actually releases grace. When you do it at the right time, in response to the Holy Spirit and in the fear of the Lord, you will discover that the Lord has been waiting to empower this kind of consecration. His heart is moved by your devotion to please Him (He views your covenant as an expression of love). If you make this covenant, you'll feel His smile as His grace rushes in and strengthens you to fulfill your vow. He's eager to help you walk in obedience!

*If an eye covenant seals shut a doorway of sin, it's not a source of bondage but freedom.*

Paul wrote, "Walk in the Spirit, and you shall not fulfill the lust of the flesh" (Gal. 5:16). The eye covenant is a tool to help you walk in the Spirit. If you have no struggles with the lust of the flesh, then this tool isn't necessary for you. But if you're like many, this eye covenant will equip you to walk in the Spirit and not fulfill the lusts of the flesh.

Vows aren't a return to legalism. Actually, they predate Moses' law because Jacob's vow came before the law was given (Gen. 28:20). They're rooted not in the era of law but the era of promise. When you invoke a vow, you enter realms of promise, faith, and grace.

Could someone potentially make a covenant with their eyes in a premature way and end up in accusation and condemnation? Yes—just as someone under a marriage vow could violate that vow and end up in accusation and condemnation. But if a married person commits adultery, we would consider it *appropriate* for them to feel some accusation and conviction. They have violated covenant!

But never would I suggest that a marriage covenant is a vehicle of condemnation! Quite the opposite, it's a vehicle of grace that empowers a couple to remain true to one another. Similarly, an eye covenant is a God-ordained means to strengthen our pursuit of holiness.

Before you make an eye covenant, ask yourself:

- Is it God's will for me to make this covenant?
- Do I believe that I'll be able to fulfill this covenant by God's grace?
- Is this the right time for me to take this vow?

Don't make a covenant with your eyes until you can answer these questions affirmatively and confidently.

I want to return to the earlier hypothetical question someone might ask, "Why would I want to increase my commitment from a resolve to a covenant, when at the resolve level I'm already under a huge load of guilt and accusation?" Here's why: Resolve took you 98% of the way up the mountain, but kept you slipping and sliding just shy of the summit; covenant has the potential to help you scale the final 2% of the mountain.

The resolve level kept you at a place where compromise was still an option. The door to your mind was still slightly ajar, keeping you at a place of repeated failure. Resolve wasn't enough to thrust you into full victory. Is it time to burn the bridges, sell all, and buy the great pearl of an eye covenant?

*Is it time to burn the bridges, sell all, and buy the great pearl of an eye covenant?*

God is extending a gracious gift. The wisdom of the ancients is being rediscovered—a return to the "old paths" that have empowered those who have gone before us. As the Lord spoke through Jeremiah, "Thus says the LORD: 'Stand in the ways and see, and ask for the old paths, where the good way is, and walk in it; then you will find rest for your souls. But they said, "We will not walk in it"'" (Jer. 6:16).

You should never feel any soulish compulsion to make an eye covenant. Do so only as you're led freely by the Holy Spirit, in the grace of our Lord Jesus. If you do take this vow, may the full strength of its blessings and holy enablement be yours!

## VOWS CAN BE ABUSED

Let me mention what may be one final objection to making an eye covenant: The fact that vows have sometimes been mishandled and abused in the past.

For example, I was told of one prominent preacher who taught his listeners to make vows regarding offerings. He used what the Bible taught about vows to seek to increase the amount of money coming to his ministry. Leaders will give account to Jesus one day for these kinds of abuses.

Vows were abused in Bible times, too. Jephthah's vow was certainly regrettable (Jdg. 11:30-40). Furthermore, Numbers 30:6 tells how to handle a woman who had bound herself with a "rash utterance." Clearly, some vows are rash and foolish.

If you ever realize that a vow you made with God was foolish, confess your foolishness to your gracious heavenly Father, ask His forgiveness, and receive His release from your unfortunate vow.

Just because vows have been abused doesn't make them wrong or inadvisable. It's still biblical to make vows to God. We just want to be sure we're making them in biblical ways.

God's grace isn't opposed to vows; rather, God's grace enables us to make vows and keep them.

Stories of vows in the Bible have inspired me to make vows of my own with God. My first covenant with God was when I confessed my faith in Christ, got baptized in water, and became a participant in His salvation. Like you, I confessed Jesus as my Lord and came into covenant with God. That was my first and—for many years—only covenant with God.

*If you've made an unfortunate vow, renounce it and receive the Lord's release.*

My second covenant came in 1981,

this time to God and my wife on our wedding day. I vowed myself to her in the presence of God and witnesses, and I thank God that by His grace I've remained true to that vow.

The third vow I made with God regarded my intimacy with Him. The Lord led me, based upon Jeremiah 30:21, to pledge my heart to draw near to Him in holiness every day of my life. I wrote in detail about this vow in my book, *Power of the Blood*.

And then I came into a fourth vow when I made a covenant with my eyes, as per Job 31:1. Vows have been a source of empowerment for me personally, and I wish the same for you.

In the next chapter, I'm going to define and describe some of the vows found in the Bible. My hope is that you'll gain from them, as I have, courage and confidence to make a covenant with your eyes.

> For the grace of God that brings salvation has appeared to all men, teaching us that, denying ungodliness and worldly lusts, we should live soberly, righteously, and godly in the present age, looking for the blessed hope and glorious appearing of our great God and Savior Jesus Christ, who gave Himself for us, that He might redeem us from every lawless deed and purify for Himself His own special people, zealous for good works (Tit. 2:11-14).

### [ For Small Groups ]

**Dig:** Do you have any reservations, biblically, about taking vows? Bring your argument to the group, and let's see what wisdom the Lord gives the group together.

**Share:** Have you made vows to the Lord in any other areas? Tell the group about it. Has it been helpful to you?

**Pray:** Express to the Lord your desperate need for His grace and help when it comes to sexual consecration. Are you ready to ask Him if He would inspire you to make a covenant with your eyes?

## NINE

# What is a Biblical Vow?

*Make vows to the LORD your God, and pay them (Psa. 76:11).*

When we speak of an eye covenant, this is new language for some people because vows aren't commonly talked about in some Christian circles. So let's back up a bit and begin the broader question, "What is a biblical vow?"

Consider this our working definition of a vow:

*A vow is a covenant that is solemnized by a verbal or written pledge and must never be violated—on pain of consequences.*

Marriage vows are a great example. Without the vows, a wedding is meaningless; with the vows, a wedding is magnificent! Bride and groom promise to reserve themselves to each other for life. And if either party violates the vow (adultery), there are very difficult and painful consequences.

In the Bible, vows were used at weddings and also in a variety of other contexts. Let's look at some of the ways vows were invoked and honored in the Bible so that we can use them properly and wisely. First of all, notice that there are two general categories of vows in the Bible: conditional and unconditional.

### CONDITIONAL VOWS

The idea of a conditional vow was basically, "God, if You'll do such-and-such, then I'll do such-and-such."

Among those who made conditional vows to God were Jacob, Jephthah, Hannah, and possibly Paul. If God answered their prayer, they were bound to fulfill their part of the vow. If God didn't answer their prayer, then they were released from the conditions.

The Old Testament had an offering called a "vow offering" (Lev. 7:16; Psa. 66:13-15). It was a sacrifice that was offered to complete a vow. Suppose someone prayed, "God, if You'll answer the request I'm making of You today, then I'll go to Jerusalem and offer a special sacrifice to You." If God answered the request, that person was obligated to make a vow offering to God.

Jonah's vow was most likely conditional (Jon. 2:9). We aren't told for sure, but the story seems to infer that his vow was possibly something like, "God, if You'll deliver me from this fish, I'll take Your message to Nineveh."

Contrary to the teaching of some, it's biblical to make conditional vows to God.

## UNCONDITIONAL VOWS

In this category, vows were to be honored no matter what circumstances might arise.

When Jacob made Joseph swear an oath that he would bury his body in Canaan (Gen. 50:4-6), Joseph promised to fulfill the oath regardless of what contingencies might arise. With or without Pharaoh's permission, Joseph was sworn to do it. It was an unconditional vow.

*It's biblical to make conditional vows to God.*

Marriage is an unconditional vow. Each spouse promises, "I'll reserve myself to you alone, no matter what happens in life. For better, for worse. In sickness, and in health."

The vow of the Nazirite (Num. 6) was an unconditional vow. Nothing was allowed to cancel or negate it.

Sometimes people would vow to serve in menial tasks in the tabernacle for a specific period of time, to help the Levites in their duties, and to show their devotion to God (Lev. 27:2) There were no conditions involved here; they were obligated to do it.

David and Jonathan made a covenant of loyalty with one another that had no conditions attached. It was an unconditional covenant for life (1 Sam. 18:3; 23:18; 2 Sam. 21:7).

In Ezra 10, the Israelites made a covenant with God to put away their pagan wives. It was unconditional—they were promising to put away their wives no matter what.

Understanding that biblical vows were both conditional and unconditional, let's now look at a few specific examples. I want to show how vows were invoked in Bible times. You will notice they pre-date the giving of the law and post-date the coming of Christ.

## JACOB'S VOW

Then Jacob made a vow, saying, "If God will be with me, and keep me in this way that I am going, and give me bread to eat and clothing to put on, so that I come back to my father's house in peace, then the LORD shall be my God. And this stone which I have set as a pillar shall be God's house, and of all that You give me I will surely give a tenth to You" (Gen. 28:20-22).

Starting his prayer with the word, "If," you can see that Jacob's vow was conditional. He basically said, "God, if You'll preserve me on this visit to Haran, and bring me back to my father in peace, then You'll be my God and I'll give You a tithe of all You give me."

God accepted the challenge and took care of Jacob. In exchange, Jacob kept his end of the bargain, sealing the vow at an altar in Shechem (Gen. 33:20).

## JEPHTHAH'S VOW

And Jephthah made a vow to the LORD, and said, "If You will indeed deliver the people of Ammon into my hands, then it will be that whatever comes out of the doors of my house to meet me, when I return in peace from the people of

Ammon, shall surely be the LORD'S, and I will offer it up as a burnt offering" (Jdg. 11:30-31).

God gave Israel victory over Ammon, and when Jephthah's only daughter came out of the doors to meet him, Jephthah let out a cry of distress because of his love for his daughter. This was a foolish vow (any vow that leads us to sin is foolish). Even though it was tragic, Jephthah still fulfilled it.[1]

## HANNAH'S VOW

Then she made a vow and said, "O LORD of hosts, if You will indeed look on the affliction of Your maidservant and remember me, and not forget Your maidservant, but will give Your maidservant a male child, then I will give him to the LORD all the days of his life, and no razor shall come upon his head" (1 Sam. 1:11).

Offering a conditional vow, Hannah prayed, "God, if You'll give me a son, I'll give him back to You."

Hannah's vow is both beautiful and amazing. Driven to desperation in her desire for a son, she prayed this utterly non-maternal prayer. (No normal mother wants to give her baby away.) But this was the vow God was waiting for. By giving Hannah a miracle boy, God would get His Samuel.

## DAVID AND JONATHAN'S COVENANT

So Jonathan made a covenant with the house of David, saying, "Let the LORD require it at the hand of David's

1 My friend Jim Tarter pointed out that Leviticus 5:4-6 says, "Or if a person swears, speaking thoughtlessly with his lips to do evil or to do good, whatever it is that a man may pronounce by an oath, and he is unaware of it—when he realizes it, then he shall be guilty in any of these matters. And it shall be, when he is guilty in any of these matters, that he shall confess that he has sinned in that thing; and he shall bring his trespass offering to the LORD for his sin which he has committed, a female from the flock, a lamb or a kid of the goats as a sin offering. So the priest shall make atonement for him concerning his sin." Jim claimed that Jephthah could have offered a sacrifice for his sin rather than sacrificing his daughter, but he didn't know about this provision because the law of Moses had been forgotten in the days of the judges. No one knew the law well enough to tell Jephthah of this provision. For us today, it's better to break a foolish vow than to keep it if it leads to a crime.

enemies." Now Jonathan again caused David to vow, because he loved him; for he loved him as he loved his own soul (1 Sam. 20:16-17).

The loyalty in this friendship is one of the brilliant jewels of the Bible. David looked for ways to honor this covenant even long after Jonathan had died.

## PAUL'S VOW

So Paul still remained a good while. Then he took leave of the brethren and sailed for Syria, and Priscilla and Aquila were with him. He had his hair cut off at Cenchrea, for he had taken a vow (Acts 18:18).

We're not told the nature of Paul's vow. Since it involved the shaving of his head, it could have been a Naziritic vow of consecration for a specific period of time. Or, it's possible that in the midst of the persecution he experienced in Corinth, he uttered a conditional vow something like, "God, if You'll preserve me in this city and enable me to return to Jerusalem after my work here is finished, then I'll do such-and-such."

## VOW VERSUS RESOLVE

A vow and a resolve aren't the same thing. A vow is a resolve taken to the highest level.

A resolve is a firm setting of the will. It involves determination and commitment. But a vow is more serious. It's a covenant, a pledge, a promise. A vow is a resolve on steroids.

The difference between the two becomes apparent when you see how failure is handled. If you resolve to do something but then fail, you receive the Lord's forgiveness, hit delete, get back up, and keep moving forward. If you break a vow, however, life comes to a full stop. Everything connected to the vow is in jeopardy. Life comes to a grinding halt because you can't see what the next step is going to be.

*A vow is a resolve on steroids.*

A resolve says, "I'm going to do my utmost, God helping me." A vow says, "I shall remain true. Oh God, help me!"

A vow leaves no room or provision for failure. In wedding vows, for example, there's no line such as, "And if I fail in this vow, please forgive me." After a wedding nobody asks their spouse, "What will we do if I should fail to keep my vows?" The question isn't even raised. A vow assumes that failure isn't an option.

Marriage vows are a sober thing—so sober, in fact, that each spouse asks themselves before the wedding, "Do I have what it takes to honor this vow?" If you're not sure you can keep the vow, then don't get married.

If you're contemplating a certain commitment and are uncertain whether to make it a resolve or a vow, go with the lesser and make it a resolve. A vow with God should be made only when you're absolutely persuaded in your heart that it's the thing to do.

Let me take you now to some important principles about biblical vows.

## SOME VOWS ARE PRECEDED BY A RESOLVE

Some vows start off as a resolve. First we resolve something with God and test drive it for a while to see how the new commitment feels. We're trying to discern how pleased God is to honor it with His enabling grace. As we continue to build a history in God, we grow in confidence. "I can do this. God is really helping me." Most resolves stay at that level, but there are those rare occasions in which the Lord invites us to upgrade our resolve to a vow.

I've experienced this personally. I arrived at my vows through a process. I've never made a vow as an instant decision or as a response on the spot to an altar call. My vows have started as resolves and then were later upgraded through the leading of the Holy Spirit. My history of victory during the resolve period bolstered my faith to believe God's grace would enable me to fulfill a vow in that area.

*Don't make a sudden, lifelong vow in the emotions of an altar call.*

When Jacob made his vow, it started with God extending

a promise; then Jacob responded by offering a vow. In a similar sense, each time the Lord has invited me to make a vow, it has been in conjunction with a Scripture. The Scripture gave me confidence that I was doing the right thing. I wrapped my fingers around the verse as confirmation that I was following the Spirit's wisdom. I recommend, therefore, that before making a vow you ask God for a verse or a promise. In the case of an eye covenant, your Scripture is Job 31:1.

## VOWS ARE VOLUNTARY

Deuteronomy 23:23 is very clear on this point. "That which has gone from your lips you shall keep and perform, for you voluntarily vowed to the LORD your God what you have promised with your mouth."

The Bible doesn't command us to make vows. So when it says in Psalm 76:11, "Make vows to the LORD your God, and pay them," we shouldn't view that verse as a command. The verse *urges* us to make vows, but doesn't *command* it.

Deuteronomy 23:22 further clarifies, "But if you abstain from vowing, it shall not be sin to you." This verse clearly says that if you choose to make no vows in your lifetime, you don't sin. You may not benefit from the power of a vow, but you don't sin. Vows are always voluntary.

## VOWS ARE RARE

A major difference between resolves and vows is their frequency in our lives. Resolves are many; vows are rare. One of the most delightful illustrations of how resolves can be abundant is by reading that famous portion of Jonathan Edwards's biography in which he lists his resolves for godly living. Do an internet search on "Jonathan Edwards resolutions," it's well worth the time. He listed around seventy resolutions that are gripping in their consecration. But they were resolves, not vows. You don't make seventy vows.

*Scripture urges but does not command vows.*

Vows are rare because of their sobriety. They're highly

valuable but extremely rare. Most saints will likely make no more than a handful of godly vows in their lifetime, if that many.

## THE BIBLE ENCOURAGES VOWS

When vows are made properly—advisedly, carefully, in wisdom and prayer, and in the Holy Spirit—the Bible commends them as desirable, beautiful, and helpful.

> Make vows to the LORD your God, and pay them (Psalm 76:11).
>
> To You the vow shall be performed (Psalm 65:1).
>
> You shall fear the LORD your God and serve Him, and shall take oaths in His name (Deut. 6:13).

The Bible encourages vows because they're helpful. Samson had a vow with his hair, and it really helped him by giving him strength to serve as a deliverer in Israel. Unfortunately, he didn't have a covenant with his eyes, and that's what took him down. The greatest kindness the Philistines ever did him was gouge out his eyes. He was so blinded by his passions and desires that he had to lose his eyes to see.

Vows are helpful to a marriage because they protect the holy institution. If tempted to commit adultery, our vows restrain us and preserve the covenant.

In the same way, vows are helpful in the pursuit of sexual consecration. If tempted by sexual sin, the covenant with our eyes restrains us and serves to preserve our purity. One reason God can encourage us to make vows is because He Himself makes vows (e.g., see Deut. 7:8, 12). You and I would be in deep trouble if God were not a God of covenant! Thank God for His covenant with us in Christ Jesus. To make vows, therefore, is God-like.

*Samson was so blinded by his passions that he had to lose his eyes to see.*

Vows are actually a medium for profound intimacy with God. He gives me His word, I give Him my word. He makes covenant with me, I make covenant with Him. He's promised to me, I'm promised to Him. The reciprocity is very affectionate.

## VOWS MAY BE TEMPORARY OR LIFELONG

Many of the vows in the Bible were only for a limited period of time. Nazirites, for example, usually vowed themselves to the Lord for a specific period of time (Num. 6). There were exceptions, mind you, such as Samson's Nazirite vow which was for life (Jdg. 13:5). It seems also that both Samuel and John the Baptist were under a lifelong Nazirite vow (1 Sam. 1:11; Luke 1:15). But most Nazirite vows were temporary.

In some instances there were conditions on a vow, and when the conditions were met, the vow was finished. This was true in Hannah's case. Once she had given Samuel to the Lord at Shiloh, she had fulfilled her vow (1 Sam. 1:24-28).

The point here is that not every vow you make must necessarily be for life. You can put a time frame on it if you like. This principle will be important in chapter thirteen when we talk about practical ways to implement an eye covenant.

## VOWS MUST BE KEPT

God keeps His vows, and He expects us to do likewise.

I'm so glad that we serve a covenant-keeping, oath-honoring, promising-fulfilling God. When God made His covenant with Abraham (Gen. 15), He never gave Himself the option to cancel it. It's in force still today. I love the fact that God is still in covenant with Abraham because that assures me He'll handle me in the same way. Once He makes a promise, He's good to His word right to the end.

The best covenant in the whole Bible is that which God has made with His only begotten Son. God has sworn amazing promises to our Lord Jesus. When He decreed to Him, "I will give You the nations for Your inheritance, and the ends of the earth for Your possession" (Psa. 2:8), you can be assured of this: Jesus *will* fully possess the hearts and minds of all His people to the very ends of the earth!

*With God, there is none of this business of making and then breaking vows.*

With God, there's none of this business of making and then breaking vows. Neither is there to be with us. This is why vows are so weighty, fearful, and few.

The fearful nature of vows is at the very center of this book's message. The terror element makes us tremble, but it also releases the covenant's power. We now turn to look at this most glorious theme—the fear of the Lord.

### [ For Small Groups ]

**Dig:** Find an account of someone in the Bible who took a vow, then tell the story to the group, along with any insights you have from it.

**Share:** Tell the group the primary thing you learned about vows from this chapter. Did you find the distinction between vows and resolves helpful?

**Pray:** Would you like to ask the Lord to grant you the courage and willingness to make vows to Him, as the Holy Spirit might direct?

TEN

# Coming Under the Terror of the Lord

*Therefore I am terrified at His presence;*
*when I consider this, I am afraid of Him (Job 23:15).*

When it comes to resisting sexual temptation, how strongly do you want your braking system to work? Do you want brakes that grab and jerk you up short when facing temptation? If you want screeching brakes—brakes that actually stop you—then you're going to have to do something violent. You're going to have to make a covenant with your eyes.

When I'm facing temptation, I want an internal alarm that drives my pancreas into my throat. I want warning lights to flash and a booming voice to thunder inside my chest, "No! I can't even give that thing a glance. I made a covenant with my eyes in the presence of God. I vowed to the Almighty that I would not look upon it, and I fear God too much to violate that vow. He's too terrifying! He's a consuming fire! His name is Jealous! I tremble at the thought of incurring His judgment. No—get behind me, Satan!"

This terror is the brake. The brake isn't the fear of sin's consequences, it's the terror of God Himself.

Your flesh actually wants to look at it. But you don't because you're just too scared. The covenant doesn't stop you from being tempted, it keeps you from considering the temptation an option. A curiosity check is now out of the question.

Strong brakes are a good thing when navigating sheer precipices.

When we realize how deadly the cliffs of sexual compromise are, we finding ourselves *wanting* a braking system that actually works. We *want* a covenant with our eyes—in much the same way that a couple wants a covenant at their wedding. Let me use the marriage covenant to illustrate.

There's something scary about a marriage covenant. You're not scared at first—you're just excited to be getting married. But then you look ahead at the vows that await you and it makes you tremble. I mean, it's scary to promise yourself to one person for the rest of your days. Once you say, "I do," you're locked in for life, no matter what life might bring. When you say, "For better, for worse," you shudder because you don't know whether life together will get better or worse. You stop and ask the hard questions, "Am I making the right choice? Will I regret this?" What's more, you know that if you violate the marriage covenant, the consequences are enormous and catastrophic. The whole prospect is terrifying.

*Strong brakes are a good thing when navigating sheer precipices.*

And still people get married. Why? Because couples *want* to come under this kind of terror. They *want* to close the door to all other options. They *want* all the traffic associated with finding and choosing a lover to be stilled. They know the covenant won't keep them from being attracted to someone else, but it will cut off the option of entertaining other attractions. They know that the only way to produce this kind of exclusive devotion is to invoke vows. They make the vows eagerly because they know the covenant will cause the fires of marital love to flourish and endure for the rest of their lives.

*Couples* want *to come under this kind of terror. They* want *to close the door to all other options.*

The same holds true with an eye covenant. We make it because we strategically and purposefully *want* to come under the terror of the Lord. We *want* it to wrap us in its sheltering arms and protect us from our mortal enemy—sin. The wise do not shun but eagerly welcome this terror. "Behold, the fear of the Lord, that is wisdom, and to depart from evil is understanding" (Job 28:28). Wisdom *wants* to crank up the fear factor.

One of the wisest things you could ever do is fuel the fear of the Lord in your life.

## WHY VOWS ARE SO FRIGHTENING

I see at least five reasons why an eye covenant is so frightening. The first is because the covenant is related to our *sexuality*. For many of us, this is the area where we most keenly feel the brokenness and vulnerability of our sinful condition. Is there any other area in our lives that has experienced similar levels of defeat, frustration, and shame? Probably not. Why, then, would we want to make a vow to God in an area characterized by some of our greatest failures? Just the idea is scary!

And that leads to the second reason why an eye covenant is so terrifying. Knowing our weakness in this area, we realize we can't possibly fulfill this covenant in the strength of our flesh or determination. We're utterly bankrupt here. The only way to keep the vow is to draw on His strength and grace every moment of every day. To be *that* dependent on God is, well, terrifying.

Thirdly, it's frightening because of the one with whom we're making the covenant. We're laying down a marker in the presence of the Almighty, the Lord of heaven's armies, the Creator of heaven and earth, who takes no pleasure in fools. When we say, "My eyes will not go beyond this line," we're not saying it to just anybody, we're saying it to *God*. To violate it is to break covenant with the all-powerful Ruler of the universe. Yikes! Who has played the fool with God and not regretted it?

Fourthly, a vow provides no room for failure. It's the same with marriage. Marriage vows don't have a clause that says, "I'll forgive you if you have an affair." In a similar sense, an eye covenant doesn't say, "If I blow it, I'll repent." Rather, it promises to remain true. At the resolve level, there is still some room for the flesh; we can repent, receive Christ's cleansing, get back up and move on. Over and over. But a vow takes it to another level. A vow insists that a failure is beyond possibility now. The constraints of the vow make you tremble.

And finally, vows are frightening because the Bible doesn't let us back out. We don't make a vow, change our mind, and back out. Once it's made, we're locked in—for as long as the vow is in force. Vows are binding, as evidenced in these passages.

> If a man makes a vow to the LORD, or swears an oath to bind himself by some agreement, he shall not break his word; he shall do according to all that proceeds out of his mouth (Num. 30:2).
>
> When you make a vow to the LORD your God, you shall not delay to pay it; for the LORD your God will surely require it of you, and it would be sin to you. But if you abstain from vowing, it shall not be sin to you. That which has gone from your lips you shall keep and perform, for you voluntarily vowed to the LORD your God what you have promised with your mouth (Deut. 23:21-23).
>
> Make vows to the LORD your God, and pay them; let all who are around Him bring presents to Him who ought to be feared (Psa. 76:11).
>
> When you make a vow to God, do not delay to pay it; for He has no pleasure in fools. Pay what you have vowed. Better not to vow than to vow and not pay (Eccl. 5:4-5).

Those are some pretty weighty passages!

When you understand the sobriety of making an eye covenant before God, it makes you tremble all the way through. This is the terror of the Lord. It's clean (Psa. 19:9), it's wise (Prov. 9:10), it's invaluable (Isa. 33:6), and it's the only way to go.

## VOWS ARE EMPOWERING

Yes, vows are terrifying. But they're also immeasurably rewarding. We see this illustrated beautifully in marriage.

Marriage vows are fearful because they're made in the presence of God. But they're also very rewarding because God becomes an active facilitator. He not only holds you to the vow, He helps you stay true. God is really into vows! He steps in, partners with you, and empowers you to remain faithful. Even when the *wicked* vow themselves in marriage, God helps them stay true. When you make the vow, God watches over it to be sure it empowers your marriage.

The same is true with your eye covenant. The vow gets God involved. He so delights in the vow that He steps in, seals your heart, and grants the grace to perform it. You realize that your desperate dependence upon Jesus is producing new levels of intimacy, affection, holiness, and power to overcome. Make an eye covenant with God in the right way, and the sense of power you feel in your walk is quite remarkable.

The natural mind thinks, "Making an eye covenant is so fearful that I would strive in the flesh to fulfill it." But here's the wonder of it—when God gets involved, the vow actually connects you to the resources of His grace. Rather than straining and striving to keep it, you find yourself empowered in the Spirit to remain true. You'll discover that His zeal to empower this eye covenant is stronger than your zeal to perform it.

*When you make an eye covenant, the sense of power you feel in your walk is quite remarkable.*

As Mary said, "His mercy is on those who fear Him" (Luke 1:50). When you tremble over your vow, His fountain of mercy enables you to keep your eyes on Christ alone.

God responds with delight to the sheer brashness of invoking His terror. Over and over in His word, He promised blessings to those who fear Him. He has promised to help them (Psa. 115:11), grant them health and strength (Prov. 3:7-8), deliver them (2 Ki. 17:39), give them honor and life (Prov. 22:4), extend their days (Prov. 10:27), take pleasure in them (Psa. 147:11), show them everlasting mercy (Psa. 103:17), and fulfill their desires (Psa. 145:19). Lord, may this terror so grip my soul that it leaves me trembling on my hands and knees in overwhelmed awe (Dan. 10:10).

Get God involved in your quest for purity and consecration. Make an eye covenant, and tap into the mercy and grace that He releases to those who tremble before Him. Your vow will terrify you—and the empowering help of the Holy Spirit will thrill you.

## "WHAT WILL HAPPEN IF I VIOLATE THE VOW?"

In the frailty of our humanity, we want to know the answer to this question. "What if I blow it? What happens then?"

Here's the scary part: Nobody can predict what will happen to you when you fall into the hands of the living God (Heb. 10:31). He whose name is Jealous is a consuming fire (Ex. 34:14; Heb. 12:29).

Violating your covenant with God works the same way as if you violate your covenant with your spouse. If you commit adultery, you place yourself entirely in the hands of your spouse. Your spouse has the right to handle you in any way he or she desires. She can divorce you, separate from you, or forgive you outright and fight for the marriage. She holds all the cards. Your adultery puts her in the driver's seat. She can handle you any way she wants.

The same is true with God. Violate a vow you've made with Him and He can respond any way He wants. He can punish you, afflict or chasten you, slap your wrist, or receive your repentance and act like it never happened.

Your vow has given Him carte blanche to respond however He wants to your infidelity.

You don't even want to go there! Don't test those boundaries. Make a covenant with God and keep it.

> *Violate a vow you've made with God and He can respond any way He wants.*

## GOD'S HISTORY WITH COVENANT BREAKERS

Nobody knows how God will respond if you violate your vow. But we can look at how He responded to people in Bible times who did so. Here are some sobering instances.

### *Achan*

God described Achan's sin as a transgression of His covenant (Josh. 7:11). God commanded the people of Israel to touch none of the plunder in Jericho, but to burn it all as an offering to Him. Achan, however, stole some of the plunder and buried it in his tent. This made God amazingly angry. God saw it as a breach of covenant, as this verses reveals:

> "Then it shall be that he who is taken with the accursed thing shall be burned with fire, he and all that he has, because he has transgressed the covenant of the LORD, and because he has done a disgraceful thing in Israel (Josh. 7:15).

What was Achan's punishment for violating covenant? Achan and his children were stoned to death, and then all his herds were burned with fire. Then they raised a heap of stones over him and all his possessions (Josh. 7:24-26). It's a dreadful example of how God responded to a covenant-breaker.

### *Samson*

Samson was in a Nazirite vow with God, and one of the conditions of the vow was that he never cut his hair. He made the mistake, however, of divulging this secret to Delilah. When she cut his hair as he slept, Samson lost his supernatural might and returned to the strength of a normal man.

The Philistines gouged out his eyes and made him a grinder of grain in prison. His ministry ended abruptly, and he became an object of the Philistines' derision and abuse. Truly Samson paid an awful price for violating his vow.

### *Jerusalem*

Jeremiah tells the consequences Jerusalem suffered for making a covenant with God and then breaking it. Oppression of Hebrew slaves was common in Jerusalem. But then Zedekiah and the people of Judah made a covenant to honor the year of jubilee. They promised God they would set all their Hebrew slaves free (Jer. 34:9), as the year of jubilee mandated.

In accordance with their covenant, they freed their Hebrew slaves. But later they changed their minds and made their slaves return (Jer. 34:10-11).

When they made a covenant and then went back on it, it really rankled God, and the consequences were dreadful. He promised to turn them over to sword, pestilence, and famine. He gave them into the hands of their enemies, the Babylonians, who burned Jerusalem and razed the cities of Judah (Jer. 34:17-22). What a price to pay for breaking covenant!

The stories of Achan, Samson, and Jerusalem make you quiver because we see that sometimes God responds in terrible ways to those who violate covenant.

However, the Bible also records times when God responded to covenant-breakers in amazing mercy. Many times when God's people were unfaithful to Him, He pled with them to return to Him, showing His willingness over and over to receive His covenant-breaking people back into His embrace. The book of Hosea shows God's merciful willingness to take back His beloved covenant-breakers. Also take a look at Ezra 10:1-3, which shows what the people of Israel did after breaking covenant with God: They returned to Him and renewed the covenant yet once more.

My point here is that God is both kind and severe (Rom. 11:22). He can respond either way, and how He chooses to respond is totally His call. The biblical record indicates that you can't know in advance how God will respond if you violate your vow. But what if you do? Tremble over your foolishness. Prostrate and throw yourself on His mercy.

Therefore, here's our conclusion: When we make covenants with God, we're going to keep them!

## COUNT THE COST

Before you make a covenant with your eyes, count the cost. Ask yourself, "Do I have what it takes to follow through and abide by this covenant for the length of its duration?"

> It is a snare for a man to devote rashly something as holy, and afterward to reconsider his vows (Prov. 20:25).

Before a couple exchanges wedding vows, they stop and consider whether they have what it takes to remain true to the vow they're about to invoke. "Am I capable of remaining true and never loving another?" They count the cost.

The same is true with an eye covenant—we must count the cost. Do we have what it takes to deliver on the covenant?

To repeat, we don't keep an eye covenant with sheer will-power. We know that we're utterly dependent upon Christ and His grace. When Christ leads us into the vow, He grants the grace to fulfill it. However, we have a role to fulfill. Christ can't do our part for us. He will extend His grace, but we must exercise our will and govern what we do with our eyes. He won't move our head or our eyes for us. We have to do that part.

So count the cost. Weigh the consequences. Ask yourself, "Am I ready to stop using certain media, or looking at certain programs?" This will impact music, videos, and computer usage—everything. If you start into it, do you have the inner resolve to complete it? Look at Jesus' advice.

> For which of you, intending to build a tower, does not sit down first and count the cost, whether he has enough to finish it—lest, after he has laid the foundation, and is not able to finish, all who see it begin to mock him, saying, "This man began to build and was not able to finish" (Luke 14:28-30).

Ask yourself, "Can I afford the risk of making a covenant before God with my eyes?"

And then ask yourself, "Can I afford *not* to make a covenant before God with my eyes?"

If you have the grace-empowered resolve to honor the covenant all the way to the end, then do it!

Somebody might say, "But I have a history of failure in this area. If I make a covenant with my eyes, how can I know it will be different?" This is an important question to ask. Take time with it. Ask the Holy Spirit, "Are You extending to me the grace to make a covenant with my eyes?"

If God's grace is being offered to you, put your confidence in His grace.

## HOW AFRAID OF GOD ARE YOU?

Do you tremble in the presence of the holiness, majesty, power, justice, and jealousy of God? You should. He's a consuming fire (Heb. 12:28-29).

He's a God who punishes sin, judges the wicked, and disciplines His children. He's to be greatly feared.

If you don't tremble before the terror of the Lord, don't make a covenant with your eyes.

I'll say it again. If the terror of the Lord doesn't make you tremble all the way through, don't make a covenant with your eyes. The whole point is to make a covenant that so terrorizes you that it brings you to a full stop in the face of temptation.

> *If you don't tremble before the terror of the Lord, don't make a covenant with your eyes.*

The last thing you want to do is make a covenant with your eyes flippantly, without fear, and then renege on the covenant because you didn't truly tremble before God.

Making a covenant with your eyes should make you tremble all over. It should scare you spitless—because you understand the gravity of coming into covenant with God.

## ASK FOR MORE

Second Corinthians 7:1 speaks of "perfecting holiness in the fear of God." The implication is that holiness and the fear of the Lord are things we grow in. So if you want more of the fear of the Lord operating in your soul, ask for more. God wants to teach you more about this fear (Ps. 34:11).

If you haven't had one yet, I suggest you ask God for an encounter with the fear of the Lord. What could be wiser than asking to be awakened to the fear of the Lord which is clean and enduring forever (Ps. 19:9)?

In my case, my awakening to the fear of the Lord happened when He chastened me. I knew from Hebrews 12:11 that His chastening is painful, but I had no idea just how painful it could be. When He disciplined me, it actually surfaced in my body in the form of a painful vocal infirmity. One tiny, gentle touch of His chastening hand sent shock waves reverberating throughout my entire being—spirit, soul, and body. It was terrifying.

And it was also glorious. He brought me into unprecedented intimacy and holiness (Heb. 12:10). Through the spirit of revelation, I began to see Jesus like never before. The encounter was painful, but now I'm so grateful He baptized me in the fear of the Lord.

*Ask God for an encounter with the fear of the Lord.*

It's heaven's kindness to grant you the fear of the Lord. It keeps, restrains, preserves, and directs us. Ask for more!

## HANDLING BUMPS

There's a difference between a covenant violation and what I call a "bump." Let me illustrate the difference from the example of marriage.

Suppose I come to my wife and say, "Sweetheart, I was tempted today with lustful thoughts toward another woman. I'm confessing this to you and am asking you to pray for me." That's a bump. She's quite willing to pray with me for that kind of thing. That's different than saying, "Honey, I slept with another woman last night, please forgive me." That's not a bump, that's a violation! She's not going to pray over a violation. That's the difference between a bump and a violation.

Applied to your eye covenant, if you flagrantly violate it, let's say, by stepping back into full-blown pornography, I don't have much counsel for you. You're in a precarious place. You'll have to work that out with God. Throw yourself on the Rock and cry for mercy.

But if you have a bump, that's different; in that case, I have some advice.

When you make a covenant with your eyes, you'll likely have bumps along the way. I'll use an illustration to show what I mean by "bumps." Let's suppose that your eyes catch a provocative magazine cover at the grocery checkout, and you immediately turn away. But then something strange takes over your head. For some crazy reason that you can't account for, your head turns back toward the rack, and your eyes take a second look. It was only a glance, but it was a second glance. That's a bump. It's illegal. It's not allowed by your covenant, but you took a second glance for some bizarre, fleshly reason. Now what do you do?

Repent quickly. "Lord, I'm sorry. Please forgive me. I don't like the fact that I took that second look. I don't want to be doing that. Please forgive me, and please help me to not do that again. I receive the cleansing of Your blood now, and Your empowering grace to enable me to overcome."

It was a bump. You regret it, and you're setting your heart to master that thing. He forgives you and helps you to keep moving forward.

God isn't a taskmaster who is about to punish you at the slightest infraction. Quite the opposite, He's a ravished Lover who is absolutely delighted in the covenant you've made. He's moved by your devotion and consecration. His heart is ravished over you (Song 4:9)!

He longs to empower you to overcome. He doesn't keep score, and He doesn't have a legal ruler by which He's measuring every action. He's for you (Rom. 8:31), and He yearns to help you find wholehearted obedience and overcoming freedom.

*He's a ravished Lover who is absolutely delighted in the covenant you've made.*

Instead of being condemned by a bump, be encouraged by how much it bothers you. Rejoice in the zeal you have to reach higher.

When you're bumping your way forward in your covenant, here's what your Beloved says to you:

> "You have dove's eyes behind your veil" (Song 4:1).

He says you have dove's eyes because your eyes are set on Him alone. All you see is Jesus. All you desire is Jesus. You've espoused your heart to Him forever.

Doves are lovebirds. They're always in pairs, they mate for life, and they do everything together. That depicts your relationship with Christ. Wherever He goes, you go. You and He are a pair of inseparable doves whose eyes are always aware of each other.

But then He adds the words, *behind your veil*. "You have dove's eyes behind your veil." Your veil is your vow. Your veil is the vow you made to not look at other affections but to reserve your heart for Jesus alone. As you peer through the veil of your vow, your eyes are covenanted to Jesus alone. With your eye covenant you have not simply said no to tempting sights; you have said yes to fixating upon the beauty and glory of Christ Jesus.

Your eye covenant touches Him at the deepest places. He's ravished by the way you've set your gaze upon Him. Let Him say it to your heart once more, "You have dove's eyes behind your veil."

### [ For Small Groups ]

**Dig:** Do a Bible study on the fear of the Lord, and share with the group the Scriptures that were most meaningful to you in the study. (You can punch in a Bible word search at a site such as www.BibleGateway.com)

**Share:** Talk about the idea of intentionally bringing ourselves under the terror of the Lord. Does this seem like wisdom to you? Talk about the difference between a violation and a bump.

**Pray:** Let's ask the Lord to help us grow in the fear of the Lord. Pray for each one in the group.

# PART FOUR

## Making the Covenant

This section will show you how to actually make a covenant with your eyes.

ELEVEN

# Why Men Need to Make a Covenant with Their Eyes

*I desire therefore that the men pray everywhere, lifting up holy hands, without wrath and doubting (1 Tim. 2:8).*

Men—you've been created by God to be activated sexually through your eye gate. And He created women in such a way that you would find them visually desirable. He did this because He wants a couple to rejoice and delight in their marriage. God designed sex to bring a husband and wife together in intimacy and affection. When a husband and wife are intimate, their relationship is strengthened and the marriage made secure.

It often starts with a man laying his eyes on a woman. "She's nice! I like her! I wouldn't mind being with her for the rest of my days."

By the way, if you're a single man and looking for a wife, it's possible to check out the beauty of a single woman without lusting for her. Just because you're looking for a wife doesn't mean you're looking lustfully upon women.

The Bible acknowledges that the eyes play a significant role in marital love, which means that God designed a man's sense of sight as a gate to open the way to the delights of marital intimacy (see Prov. 5:18-19; Song 4:9; 8:10).

For men with same-sex attraction, it also starts with the

eyes. Regardless of the orientation, the eye is the gate.

Men, if you find women physically attractive, God made you like that. He made you to desire, and He made women desirable. When God built these feelings into our sexuality, He called it "very good" (Gen. 1:31). It's normal and right for women to long to be loved and to be admired as beautiful. And it's normal and right for men to admire their beauty.

Here's the bad part. Sin ruined everything. In the garden, our sexuality took a devastating hit, and now there's no other area in which we feel the fallout from sin more deeply and immediately. In the struggle with sin, the primary area of struggle for many men is in their sexuality. Sin warped and bent our ability to function sexually as God intended, and now we're prone to lust and temptation.

*Regardless of the orientation, the eye is the gate.*

> Hell and Destruction are never full; so the eyes of man are never satisfied (Prov. 27:20).
>
> For all that is in the world—the lust of the flesh, the lust of the eyes, and the pride of life—is not of the Father but is of the world (1 Jo. 2:16).

In speaking with Cain, God described every man's battle. He described sin as something that lies at the door of our lives and wants to devour us, but we have a mandate to rule over that temptation (Gen. 4:7). Since the eye is the door to our sexuality, we must now exercise mastery over the sin that wants to gain entrance at the doorway of the eyes.

If your eye gate is open, you'll look upon the woman and begin to fantasize sinfully. If your eye gate is closed, the image is cut off at the gate, and now you can contend for mastery over your thought life.

This is why men should make a covenant with their eyes. Through this covenant, the Holy Spirit gives us the power to close the door of our eyes to the lustful images that desire entrance. With the eye gate shut, we can engage in the glorious pursuit of bringing every thought into obedience to Christ (2 Cor. 10:5).

When you make an eye covenant, you appreciate when your sisters in Christ fight for your purity by guarding how they dress. Men, return the favor. Fight for their eye consecration by wearing clothes that are modest and well-fitting.

Both men and women can use their eyes to flirt. An eye covenant closes the door for a man or woman to all flirting. You can't flirt with the wrong person and preserve your eye covenant. When a woman tries to catch your eye and communicate her interest with her eyes, your soul will be like a sealed wall. You will immediately turn away.

*With the eye gate shut, we can engage in the glorious pursuit of bringing every thought into obedience to Christ.*

Your eye covenant will be kept only as you draw upon the power and help of the Holy Spirit. He abides within, and is always present to help in times of need. He rushes to empower your consecration because He takes great delight in strengthening this covenant. Call on the help of the indwelling Christ!

## IMPLICATIONS

When a man makes an eye covenant, it's amazing how many areas of his life are affected on a practical level by one single vow. The eyes change everything! The following isn't intended as a "list of do's and don'ts," but as a guide to help you understand how your eye covenant is so all-encompassing. These things may not be actually written into your vow, but when you make an eye covenant here are just some of the things you'll probably mean your covenant to include:

- I will not allow my eyes to take a second look at a woman that I find attractive and stimulating.
- I will not allow my eyes to take a second look at a seductive picture.
- I will not watch a movie that might have arousing scenes, and if I'm caught off guard by a movie, I will walk out or turn it off.

- I will not continue to watch a TV program when it turns seductive or uses sexual humor.
- I will not click on a link that might be sexually suggestive.
- I will never intentionally do an internet search that might produce arousing options.
- I will never look twice at the tabloid covers located at the grocery store checkout counter or on the magazine rack.
- I will not scope the bodies sunbathing on the beach.
- I will never check out pay-per-view options.
- I will not surf through the TV channels in the hopes of "accidentally" seeing some skin.
- I will never visit a porn shop.
- I will not go to a dining establishment where the servers are dressed provocatively.
- I will never call 900-code sex lines.
- I will not enter airport magazine stores that feature provocative covers.
- I will not visit red light districts.
- When in a hotel, I will not call for an in-room massage.
- I will not touch a woman in an inappropriate way.
- I will not hang out voluntarily in social contexts with men who verbalize their lust (understanding that some exposure on the job may be involuntary).
- I will never flirt with a woman other than my wife.
- I will not tell jokes that carry sexual innuendo.
- I will not wear clothes that lack modesty.
- I will not look at newspapers or magazines in which women model underwear or bathing suits.
- I will not look upon sensual TV commercials.
- I will not send or receive provocative text messages.
- I will not be friends with an ex-girlfriend on social media.
- I will not listen to the smooth words of anyone trying to seduce me.

- I will use the strength of my eyes and mind to focus on the pursuit of the knowledge of Christ.

The beauty and wisdom of an eye covenant is the way it addresses so many scenarios with one simple statement, "I have made a covenant with my eyes." Other approaches to purity often become complicated. For example, some books will tell you what to do in this situation; and then what to do in that situation; and then what to do in another situation—as though every possible scenario needs to have its own unique solution. The Bible has made it easy for us by giving us the tool of an eye covenant. Just devote yourself to this one sweeping covenant and boom, the host of sexual temptations that seek entrance to your mind are addressed and thwarted. What a gift!

> If then you were raised with Christ, seek those things which are above, where Christ is, sitting at the right hand of God. Set your mind on things above, not on things on the earth. For you died, and your life is hidden with Christ in God (Col. 3:1-3).

### [ For Small Groups ]

**Dig:** Take one of the verses mentioned in this chapter and study it in its context. Bring your findings to the group.

**Share:** Tell the group why you think men should make a covenant with their eyes.

**Pray:** Gather in clusters of two or three. Express to each other what about the eye covenant might be challenging, troubling, or drawing you, and then pray for each other.

TWELVE

# Why Women Need to Make a Covenant with Their Eyes

*Do not let your adornment be merely outward—arranging the hair, wearing gold, or putting on fine apparel—rather let it be the hidden person of the heart, with the incorruptible beauty of a gentle and quiet spirit, which is very precious in the sight of God (1 Pet. 3:3-4).*

Let me start this chapter with a story. As part of my preparation for writing this book, I met with a small group of women and asked them quite bluntly, "How does a woman's sexuality work? I understand male sexuality because I am one, so it's easy for me to write to men. But I don't pretend to understand female sexuality. How do I write to women?"

I explained to them what I meant. I explained that the gate to a man's sexuality is the eye, and that if a man closes the eye gate, he deals a decisive blow to sexual temptation right where it tries to start. When a man makes a covenant with his eyes, he's closing the gate to his sexuality, getting the temptation on the outside of his castle, and now he can fight for sexual consecration from a place of advantage.

So my big question to the women was, "If the eye is the gate to a man's sexuality, what is the gate to a woman's sexuality? To say it another way, if a man makes a covenant with his eyes in order to close the door to temptation, with what does a woman make a covenant? What door must a woman shut?"

At first the women said, "A woman's gate is her mind." But I challenged that idea. The mind is not a woman's gate; the mind is a woman's center. It's the interior of the castle. The mind is the engine of our sexuality, for both women and men. If the mind is the interior of the castle where sexuality is centered, what is the castle gate? What is the primary door that activates a woman's fantasies? With what gate should a woman make a covenant?

As they continued to discuss the question, they suddenly came to the same conclusion: "The gate for a woman is the same as for a man. The primary gate to a woman's sexuality is the eye." A woman's temptation to fantasy, they agreed, is fed primarily through data coming to her eyes.

The conclusion, therefore, was that women also need to make a covenant with their eyes.

This conclusion stunned me. One reason I wasn't expecting that answer was because I had read a claim by one author that women were triggered primarily by their ears (hearing). So I thought perhaps the women would conclude that their gate was the ears or perhaps touch or even smell. I was totally taken aback when they concluded, "The gate for women is the same as for men. It's the eyes." Hearing, touch, and smell certainly play a role as secondary gates, but the eyes are the primary trigger. As they told me this, I suddenly realized that the invitation of Job 31:1 is universal—it's for the entire body of Christ. The power of an eye covenant is available to *everybody*.

*The mind is the center of our sexuality, not the gate.*

I wanted to be sure, however, that their conclusion would bear the scrutiny of others. So I met with another group of women. I also sent out a raft of emails to get long-distance input, and almost everyone agreed with this conclusion. The opinions I've received have come from women who were single, married, younger, and older. The content of this chapter is based, not on my personal opinions or conclusions, but entirely upon the input I received from this diverse group of women.

The first observation I need to make is that there's no uniform or universal way that women are triggered in their sexuality. In this chapter, I'm going to address what seemed to be characteristic of the majority of women, but when it comes to sexuality there are always exceptions. Women on the whole are more complex in their responses than men. Therefore, please do not read this chapter as a dogmatic statement on every woman's sexuality. Far from it! I still don't have a clue about female sexuality. I'm simply going to do my best to reflect the input I received from the women who gave me feedback.

*There's no uniform or universal way that women are triggered in their sexuality,*

If you're a woman, please don't be thrown off by something in this chapter that may not fit you. Rather, ask God to speak to you from the spirit of Job 31:1, and then allow Him to personalize the message of this book for you.

Here's the main point I'm boldly proclaiming in this chapter: Women also need to make a covenant with their eyes.

While the other gates of hearing, touch, and smell also operate in women, the *primary* gate to a woman's sexuality is the eye. The eye is the gate, and the mind is the mainframe where fantasies swirl and emotions incubate. The eyes function as the gate because most of the traffic in a woman's thought life starts from data that enters through the eyes. When a woman makes an appropriate covenant with her eyes, she is able to seal her heart from incoming visual data that wants to touch her vulnerabilities, and then she can begin the magnificent task of "bringing every thought into captivity to the obedience of Christ" (2 Cor. 10:5).

That women should make a covenant with their eyes is a new idea for some. I need to take the time, therefore, to explain why it's helpful. My hope is that women reading this chapter will be able to identify how their eye gate works, and be emboldened to adopt a covenant with their eyes.

## HOW DOES A WOMAN'S EYE GATE FUNCTION?

Although the main gate to a woman's sexuality is the same as a man's, how it functions is often quite different. Women are not wired like men. Men look on the female form and feel sexual desire; but most women aren't aroused simply by looking on the male form. Mind you, there are exceptions. Many women today are users and even addicts of pornography, much more today than prior to the internet. Exposure to pornography from childhood can even give women eyes for other women. Women who struggle with sexual addictions will find a covenant with their eyes powerfully liberating.

Most women, however, do not struggle with looking lustfully upon men's bodies. The way the eye of women works has largely to do with *comparisons*.

## COMPARISONS

Women have been created by God with a strong desire to be beautiful. It's healthy and normal for a woman to fix herself up nicely, and for a wife to want to look attractive to her husband. Sin has distorted that normal desire, however, and now women are susceptible to envy, covetousness, self-hatred, lust, and pride, even to the point of using seduction and manipulation for selfish gain.

*The eye gate for women is triggered largely by comparisons.*

Women tend to look at other women and compare themselves. They try to be attractive to men, but they sometimes measure their attractiveness by comparing themselves to the appearance of other women.

Sometimes they will survey the group until their eyes land on the woman they consider most attractive, and then the comparisons begin.

"I would kill to have your legs."

"What is it like to look like that?"

"The way you walk makes me mad."

Or, on the flip side, a woman might look in a condescending way upon a woman who is considered less attractive.

"Exercise! Do something about that."

Women can sometimes feel the power they have over others when they're being noticed. Some women actually derive their sense of identity from how others notice them.

Some women get dressed to be noticed. "How will I look to them in these clothes?" A woman can make an agreement in her heart, as she's putting on her clothes, that she intends to get noticed that day.

Many women do want to be noticed by men, but often their first thought is how they will appear to other women. Women look at other women. Some don't dress primarily for men; they dress for other women. It's not that they're trying to arouse other women, though that may be the case for a few; it's that they're wanting to make women a little envious, or hoping to gain their admiration.

*Some women get dressed to get noticed.*

This is not true for all, of course. Women can, in a healthy and God-honoring way, enjoy sharing fashion delights with each other, encouraging, complimenting, and edifying one another in the beauty of their identity in Christ. The temptation for comparisons proceeds from a healthy feminine quality that has been distorted by our fallenness.

A woman can compare husbands. Perhaps she sees or hears of something another man did for his wife. Those comparisons can tempt her to imagine how much better her life might be under different circumstances. Perhaps that other man could love, satisfy, and provide for her more than her husband. Perhaps a different lifestyle would bring her more happiness. Something inside says she deserves something better. Initially, her fantasies might be more romantic than sexual as her mind writes the script of what life might look like with him.

Mind you, men are tempted to compare wives and fantasize about what it might be like to be married to someone else. When it comes to comparing and coveting spouses, men and women alike need a covenant with their eyes because they are equally susceptible.

A woman wants a man who will appreciate her, believe in her, partner with her, care for her, and be a life companion. This is what the eye looks for. The eye can fall on another woman's husband, or on someone other than her own husband, and fantasies can begin.

If a young woman's eye gate is open, she can look to men for affirmation and value instead of to Christ. Once her eyes are on a man, she becomes vulnerable to his kind words. When he says, "You are special, you deserve the best, I love you," the emptiness in her soul opens her to temptation.

Many affairs get started by the exchange that takes place with eye contact. Perhaps she catches the eye of a man and he starts to show his appreciation. "Do the people in your life know how great you are?" he asks. If she's feeling stuck and bored, the fantasies can tumble and the compliments can flush her cheeks. It often starts with an eye exchange, and then the emotions swirl with the conversations that follow.

## COMPETING WITH AN INDUSTRY

Women often feel pressure to compete with the images that the fashion industry models. How do you keep up with the skin of a seventeen-year-old? Catering to the desire of women to recover their youthfulness, entire industries have arisen that enable women to undergo a host of medical procedures to enhance their attractiveness.

There's quite an amazing array of procedures available today, if you can afford them. You can make a certain part of the body larger, or smaller, or smoother. You can get Botox injections. Lasers. Liposuction sculpting. Tummy tucks. Implants. Breast reductions or enhancements. Lifts. Collagen. Nose jobs. Tooth whiteners. Dermabrasion. Sclerotherapy. Chemical peel. Eyelid lifts. Facelifts. Lip augmentation.

These industries are often fueled by the fear of aging. Women look at their bodies and see how their physical beauty is fading with the years. It's unfortunate how the beholding of the physical body can cause a woman to lose perspective on that which is truly valuable—the inner beauty of a gentle and quiet spirit. She can serve Christ faithfully for years growing graciously in the likeness of Christ, and then lose sight of that inner treasure because of discouragement over her fading physique. The glory of the indwelling Christ gets dwarfed by the talking mirror.

Our culture doesn't give women the permission to age. Something that should be celebrated (the regal beauty of a woman's crowning years) is turned into a competition to try to look seventeen again. Moms compete with daughters.

## COVETOUS DESIRES

A woman can get hit with covetous thoughts simply by flipping through something as innocent as a magazine or catalog. The eye compares what is seen with what one possesses. Or it can happen while clicking through Facebook—comparing herself to someone else's photo or post.

The eyes look at what another has and it fuels jealousy. "She probably has such a great boyfriend because she's skinny." "They make a perfect couple—why am I still single?" "Look at their beautiful children, and their picture-perfect house." "It must be nice to be married to a man with a career like that." The eyes are attracted to something; then, as the eyes linger upon it, the incoming data sets up residence in the mind, and that's where it turns into jealousy, daydreaming, and fantasy.

> *The glory of the indwelling Christ gets dwarfed by the talking mirror.*

Women are often tempted, when in a store, to see stuff they don't have and covet. That same mechanism—to see and desire—also operates in the area of sexuality. For example, women look at the features of other women and covet. They covet the power with men and women that comes with being beautiful and attractive.

A woman's eye gate is often activated in the bathroom when she gets herself ready in the morning. She says to the mirror, "You look disgusting." Things churn inside her when she looks at the bathroom scale.

A woman can stare mindlessly at a magazine cover at the

grocery checkout and hardly realize that her thoughts have been taken hostage by what she laid her eyes upon. This is why an eye covenant can be helpful.

The purpose of the eye covenant is not to turn women into boring religious robots who have no color in their lives; it is to sanctify their eyes to Jesus so that their true inner beauty radiates with holy joy.

## USING THE EYES

We know from Scripture that a woman can use her eyes to try to snare a man (Prov. 6:25; 2 Ki. 9:30; Isa. 3:16). She can use them in an intentional way, letting a man across the room know that she is noticing him and interested in him.

A woman can also communicate with her eyes in a way that may initially be unintentional and innocent. Her eyes can gush with appreciation for the way he inspires her, and she may not even realize the openness she is conveying.

Many affairs start in innocence. It can start with something as innocent as visiting together, or receiving counsel, or praying together, or sharing in the word. He sees in her someone who needs his help. The context is warm, caring, and interactive; faces are open to each other, hearts are transparent, and eyes are connecting.

At first she may not be thinking sex at all. She's thinking about care, comfort, trust, communication, and companionship. Her eyes draw from his eyes the care she needs. In the warmth of the friendship, her sexuality can morph from inactive to relaxed to susceptible to longing. He wants it to become physical, and she becomes vulnerable. The brakes of the terror of the Lord are not operational for either one.

Many affairs start with a man and woman entering into a relationship innocently, with no thought of sex in their minds. Eventually their eye gates become awakened to each other. If they don't have a covenant with their eyes, the relationship can get past their gate and into their heart. When emotional fulfillment produces security in the relationship, the desire for physical intimacy often comes next.

## CLOSE THE GATE

The things mentioned in this chapter are just *some* of the ways the eye gate is triggered for a woman. When the gate isn't sealed shut, the eyes can look with longing and the heart can open to fantasies.

This is why a woman should make a covenant with her eyes—in order to bring all this inner traffic to a halt. She can't truly love God with all her mind until the carnal comparisons and desires filling her mind are stilled. When the gate is closed shut, and the eyes are set straight ahead on the Lord Jesus, the things that feed fantasy, envy, and covetousness are starved out. With the eye gate closed, the other gates (hearing, touch, smell) can be easily closed as well. Now the enemy is on the outside of the castle, and the fight for a consecrated thought life can be fought from a place of advantage.

*When emotional fulfillment produces security in the relationship, the desire for physical intimacy often comes next.*

## IMPLICATIONS

When a woman makes a covenant with her eyes, it affects so many areas of everyday life. The eyes change everything! Again, the following isn't a "list of do's and don'ts." These are intended to show how making an eye covenant impacts a wide range of behaviors and attitudes. Here are just some of the things a woman will probably mean her covenant to include:

- I will look to Christ for my identity, not in how I compare to other women, or how a man shows his appreciation.
- I will prefer other women in the way I dress, so as not to provoke comparisons.
- I will fight for the consecration of my brothers in Christ through the way I dress, so it's easier for them to love God.
- I will not compare myself to the physical appearance of other women.

- I will weigh myself only when needed for health reasons and not as a means to measure beauty.
- I will not draw conclusions about other women based on what they look like.
- I will never talk or use my eyes in a way that could be considered flirtatious or sexually suggestive.
- I will not gossip or slander others.
- I will not read novels or materials that feed the tendency to fantasize.
- I will not watch TV programs or movies that produce fantasy.
- I will never view pornography, on the internet or elsewhere.
- I will never open tabloids or magazines that feed a comparing eye or that promote sexual thoughts.
- I will not touch a man in an inappropriate way.
- I will remove myself from voluntary social contexts in which the conversation promotes carnal comparisons or sexual fantasy (understanding that some exposure on the job may be involuntary).
- I will not express humor that carries sexual innuendo.
- (for wives) I will not contact an ex-boyfriend on social media.
- (for wives) I will not use my eyes to encourage any man other than my husband.
- I will use the strength of my eyes and mind to focus on the pursuit of the knowledge of Christ.

"Finally, brethren, whatever things are true, whatever things are noble, whatever things are just, whatever things are pure, whatever things are lovely, whatever things are of good report, if there is any virtue and if there is anything praiseworthy—meditate on these things" (Phil. 4:8).

## [ For Small Groups ]

**Dig:** Can you think of any verses or stories in the Bible that seem to support the idea that the eyes are the first gate to a woman's sexuality? Perhaps start with Genesis 39:7.

**Share:** Tell the group why you think women should make a covenant with their eyes.

**Pray:** Gather in clusters of two or three. Express to each other what about the eye covenant might be challenging, troubling, or drawing you, and then pray for each other.

THIRTEEN

# Practical Advice

*Meditate on these things; give yourself entirely to them, that your progress may be evident to all (1 Tim. 4:15).*

We're almost ready to write our eye covenant. We're going to do that in the next chapter, but first I want to cover some practical areas, just to be sure that we're fully ready for the covenant.

For starters, this covenant is specifically for those who have truly been born again by the Spirit of God. Before you consider a covenant with your eyes, be sure that you're in right standing with God. How do you do that? Confess your sins (Jam. 5:16), repent (Acts 2:38), receive the forgiveness of Christ (1 John 1:9) and the cleansing of His blood (Heb. 10:22). If you need help to take these steps, find a strong believer who can review these Scriptures with you and instruct you in receiving God's forgiveness.

If you're a child of God, but have been struggling with feelings of shame and failure related to sexual purity, you want to receive fresh cleansing of your conscience through the blood of Christ (Heb. 10:19-22), before you make the eye covenant. I suggest that you offer the following prayer right now.

> Our Father in heaven, I come to You in the name of Jesus Christ, and ask You to forgive me for all the immorality and

perversion I've practiced. [Confess your specific sins here.] Please forgive me for the way I've opened myself to sexual sin and to breaking Your heart. Wash me now, I pray, with the blood of Christ that He shed at Calvary, and let that precious blood cleanse my eyes, my mind, my body, and my spirit. Forgive me, Jesus. Wash me. Renew me. Restore me to fellowship with You. Make me a new person in You. Lord, I turn my back on all my old sins, and turn my face toward You to walk in obedience. In Jesus' name, I renounce and shut every door to darkness, and today I open new doors—doors of righteousness, doors of revelation, doors of light and truth. Satan, I command you, in the name of Jesus, to leave my mind, my soul, and my life. Jesus, You're now the Master of my life. I surrender my entire life to You, to walk in obedience to Your word, by the power of the Holy Spirit. Thank You for Your help!

I want to declare the great news of our glorious gospel in Christ Jesus: God forgives *all* your sexual sins! When you confess and completely turn away from your sins, He forgives them with abundant joy and acceptance. You're clean! There's no such thing as a sexual sin beyond His forgiveness. The only thing God waits for is your repentance.

Rejoice in the new start God is giving you today! The Scripture says, "As far as the east is from the west, so far has He removed our transgressions from us" (Psa. 103:12). When you stand before Him at the last day, He will act as though those forgiven sins didn't even happen. What great news! Jesus restores you to the purity of virginity (as explained in chapter four), and invites you to make a covenant with your eyes. He's leading you forward in His great victory.

**THE FIRST STEP**

If you would like to move forward with making a covenant with your eyes, let's talk about how to do that in wisdom. It's possible that someone might be ready to make a lifetime covenant with their eyes right now, and if so, that's wonderful. However, I expect that many believers are going to walk toward it in an unfolding process.

To start, consider making a covenant with your eyes for

the next twenty-four hours. (It's biblical to make a vow for a limited period of time, as explained in chapter nine.)

*To start, consider making a covenant with your eyes for the next 24 hours.*

"Heavenly Father, right now I make a covenant before You with my eyes for a day. For the next twenty-four hours, I vow to not look upon a man or woman to lust. I promise to not allow my eyes to rest upon anything displeasing to You. I set my eyes on You alone. Help me fulfill this vow, I pray, in Jesus' name."

Here's the wisdom in launching with a temporary vow: It gives you the opportunity to try on the new garment and see how it wears. Give it a test drive. You can do it for a day and then evaluate. How did the Lord help you and give you strength? Were you aware of His enabling grace?

One of the definitions of grace is enabling power. When God's grace is operating in your life, you may not be excited by any emotional feelings, but you'll realize at the end of the day that you had the strength to overcome to the end. That's grace. Don't go by feelings, just keep leaning on His help.

And talk to God throughout the day. This is what He's really looking for. He wants us to walk out the journey with Him *relationally*. The Holy Spirit lives inside of you as a flaming fire—talk to Him. Thank Him for empowering you with self-control ( Gal. 5:22-23). Talk to Jesus, who is abiding in you and walking with you each step of the way. Stay in His word and get your body filled with light. The whole point of the journey into obedience is to grow in love.

After honoring your eye vow for a day, would you like to make another vow? Perhaps for another day, or for three days? Perhaps you'll soon find yourself desiring to make a vow for a week. Then for a month. Then six months. Then a year.

When you get to the point of making a vow with your eyes for a year, and you discover the empowering grace of Christ for that year, you may be ready to make a lifetime vow of consecration with your eyes. I recommend this kind of incremental consecration as a wise way for you to work your way toward a lifetime vow. With each step in the journey, expect to be amazed at how eagerly God helps you. As said already, He's really into covenant!

## WAIT TILL YOU'RE READY

Don't make any kind of vow with God until you're completely persuaded it's the thing to do. This is repetitive, but I want to caution you against making any kind of vow prematurely, or else the adversary will try to use your weakness against you. If you have a failure, he'll hit you with a barrage of condemnation and guilt. He'll tell you that you're under the wrath of God. He'll tell you that you're an abject failure and disqualified from useful service in the kingdom of God.

I'm describing how the adversary comes against us because the Scripture says, "Lest Satan should take advantage of us; for we are not ignorant of his devices" (2 Cor. 2:11). He uses the same tricks on all of us.

The purpose of the vow is to equip you for wholehearted consecration and unprecedented victory—don't allow an impetuous decision to turn the vow into a vehicle for self-condemnation and despair. Wait, therefore, until the covenant can be a tool that empowers you rather than a chain that submerges you. When the time is right, the Holy Spirit will fill you with confidence and give you the divine go-ahead.

Don't make a covenant with your eyes if you're still manifesting addictive behavior with sexual sin, or are still bound in shame or despair. Seek the Lord for grace to become more stable in your resolve, and then consider the covenant after a season of greater stability.

> *Don't allow an impetuous decision to turn the vow into a vehicle for self-condemnation and despair.*

Don't make a covenant with your eyes if you still want to indulge your flesh with the occasional look.

Don't make a covenant with your eyes if you're not interested in changing what kinds of movies you watch.

Don't make a covenant with your eyes

if you lack the faith to believe God is really with you in this.

Don't make a covenant with your eyes if you need more time to process and ponder this divine invitation. Just as a season of engagement precedes a wedding, a season of contemplation will usually precede the vows we make with God. Wait till you're ready.

## USE THE FULL RANGE OF PURITY TOOLS

An eye covenant is just one tool among many that we should use in our pursuit of consecration. This war is so intense that we want to use every grace-empowered weapon we can get our hands on. Here are some other tools that are available to you.

***Pray the word:*** The word of God is your sword (Eph. 6:17). Use the word to take on your adversary. Collect the verses that are empowering your walk right now, and recite those Scriptures in the moment of temptation just like Jesus did (Mat. 4:4-10). The word builds your faith (Rom. 10:17), and faith is your shield against the enemy's flaming arrows (Eph. 6:16). As you're aggressive in the word and prayer, your mind will be renewed (Rom. 12:2) and your spirit made strong (Eph. 6:10). Ephesians 6:10-17 talks about putting on the full armor of God, and then the next verse (v.18) tells you what to do once you're clothed in the armor: You should pray in the Spirit. Use the word to fill your body with light, and then pray in the Spirit to get your heart vibrant in the love of Christ.

*We want to use every grace-empowered weapon we can get our hands on.*

***Meditate on Christ:*** With Ephesians 1:17-19 open in front of you, ask the Father to give you a revelation of the beauty of Jesus Christ. Spend time beholding Jesus in His word. We become what we behold. If we set our gaze on porn, we become filled with lust; if we set our gaze upon Christ, we become filled with His light and are transformed into His image (2 Cor. 3:18). Spend as much time as you can in the word, gazing on Jesus in worship and adoration. This is the main way you'll bring every thought captive to the obedience of Christ.

***Fast:*** Fasting is a glorious gift from God that enables us to accelerate our progress in the fight. When Adam ate the fruit, he took a crushing blow to his sexuality. The Bible, therefore, seems to make a connection between the appetites of our stomach and the appetites of our sexuality. Thus, fasting is a God-ordained tool to help us overcome sexual brokenness. Denying the normal appetites of our stomach actually strengthens our resolve to deny sinful sexual appetites. Furthermore, fasting tenderizes your heart to spiritual truth, increasing your understanding of the word.

***Find an accountability partner:*** Find someone who is willing to serve you, in accordance with James 5:16, as an accountability partner. That person needs to be of your gender, and preferably older than you and/or more mature in Christ than you. Find someone who will lift you up, not someone who struggles with the same problems. If you're a pastor, consider finding another pastor. Get together weekly and report how you're doing.[1] Confess everything. Confess your failures to God first, and then immediately to this person and receive prayer. Something powerful happens when we confess and receive prayer: God heals us (Jam. 5:16). Even the very pathways etched into the brain from habitual sins can be healed, releasing us from addictive behaviors of our past.

1 Before praying for one another, accountability partners can ask these suggested questions of each other:

a. Did you do anything to violate your eye covenant this past week?
b. Did you have a "bump" this week—that is, a situation in which you didn't violate your eye covenant, but in which you were not pleased with your response?
c. Have you looked at a man or woman in an inappropriate way?
d. Have you honored the Lord with your use of media this week (internet, movies, music, etc.)?
e. Have you been above reproach this week in your financial dealings, with your tongue (language), and in all relationships?
f. Have you spent time with the Lord daily in the secret place (word and prayer)? Have you honored your sabbath?
g. Have you been obedient and faithful to the Lord's call on your life?

For more input on how to maintain an effective accountability relationship, go to www.cmaresources.org and look at the Life Transformation Groups model that Neil Cole has developed.

***Repent:*** Repent immediately and wholeheartedly of every failure and sin. Receive the cleansing of the blood of Jesus, and receive His power to change. Use Psalm 51 in your repentance.

***Make no provision for the flesh:*** Romans 13:14 says, "But put on the Lord Jesus Christ, and make no provision for the flesh, to fulfill its lusts." What that means is, don't place yourself in a position to be tempted. Go through all your books, magazines, DVDs, CDs, music, etc., and throw out anything that could trigger any temptation. Ask God to show you what to keep. Rid your living space of anything defiling. Don't go to any places, such as bars, where you could be tempted. Never plan an excursion that you know will provide you with temptation. Don't look at people below the shoulders. Don't hang out with any "friends" who pressure you to compromise your vow. (If they pressure you to compromise, they're not really your friends.) Remove social media contacts that post impure topics and images. Aggressively tackle the media monster, it really wants to eat you alive. Turn the TV off after 7:00 p.m. Get accountability and filtering software for your computer (e.g., www.covenanteyes.com). Beware of channel surfing. Cancel cable TV. (A Christian needs divine permission to subscribe to Cable TV because of its many traps. Unless God gives you specific permission for certain good purposes, cancel it.)

*Something powerful happens when we confess and receive prayer: God heals us.*

There are many resources available in the body of Christ for those seeking to strengthen their sexual consecration. See the Appendix (page 142) for a sampling of books, sites, and ministries that are devoted to equipping the body of Christ for purity. These kinds of resources are always being updated, so do an internet search for the latest resources.

## A HELPFUL PRAYER

David gave us a marvelous prayer in Psalm 139:23: "Search me, O God, and know my heart." As I've offered that prayer to the Lord, I've changed the wording just a little and prayed it this way: "Lord, know me in my sexuality."

I urge you to pray that same prayer with sincerity: "Lord, know me in my sexuality." When you offer that prayer, open your arms to Him and expose your entire being to His searching eyes. When you do, you're saying, "Jesus, I lay bare before You every aspect of my sexuality. My needs, my desires, my thoughts, my struggles, my practices. Everything. Search every part. I have no secrets. Know the areas in which I'm strong and overcoming. Know the areas in which I'm weak and failing. Know my fantasies. I hide nothing from You. I invite You to search out and address any aspect of my sexuality, at any time. I'm Yours. Know me."

Never hide anything.

I'm passionate about this prayer because, on the final day when eternal destinies are being assigned, Jesus will say to some, "I never knew you; depart from Me, you who practice lawlessness!" (Mat. 7:23). I don't ever want to hear those words! I want Him to know every part of me so thaton the final day He says, "I know you, Bob."

*Never hide anything.*

Both Simon Peter and Judas Iscariot failed Jesus Christ miserably. One ended up in hell, the other became an apostle of the Lamb. What was the difference between them? Judas had secrets, Peter had none.

Never try to hide your sin from God.

Be like Peter—an open book. "Know me in my sexuality."

## KNOW YOUR VESSEL

Ask the Lord to show you where you're strong and where you're weak. When you identify your sexual vulnerabilities, you're doing what Paul wrote about:

> For this is the will of God, your sanctification: that you should abstain from sexual immorality; that each of you should *know how to possess his own vessel in sanctification and honor*, not in passion of lust, like the Gentiles who do not know God (1 Thess. 4:3-5).

In speaking of your "vessel," Paul was referring to the entirety of your person, with particular emphasis on your body. To "possess" your vessel means to be a careful guardian of your body and heart. God holds you responsible to keep your body in sanctification and honor. To do that, it's necessary that you understand your frame. You should be especially wise to the ways temptation wants to take advantage of your weaknesses.

Identify the things that make you vulnerable to sinful desires—such as being fatigued, or feeling relaxed and confident, or feeling discouraged, or lonely, or stressed. Know your danger zones—such as certain kinds of music, or movies, or places, or companions, or parties, or being alone with someone in a car, or having alcohol, etc.

Know your vessel. Then write a covenant for your eyes that will help you possess your vessel. The Lord is eager to help you—just ask Him.

## PREPARE FOR QUESTIONS

After you make your eye covenant, consider how you'll speak of it to others. People are likely to ask you questions such as, "Why won't you come with us to that movie?" "Why do you always look away when you see an attractive man or woman?" People are likely to notice the changes in your behavior, and they'll be curious.

The reason you might consider in advance how you'll respond is because it's very easy, when words are formulated casually or suddenly, to come across in a "holier than thou" or "pharisaical" manner. Ask the Lord to help you speak of your vow in a way that makes it desirable to others, rather than in a way that trumpets your spirituality.

Perhaps you would be ready to answer in ways similar to this:

"The Lord is calling me to be extra careful right now about the things I watch."

"I just don't want to view things like that."

"I read a review on that movie, and there are some things in that movie I don't want to watch because of a commitment I've made with God."

## [ For Small Groups ]

**Dig:** Meditate prayerfully in 1 Thessalonians 4:3-5, and then ask God to show you your vulnerabilities. Write down what He shows you.

**Share:** Talk about the process of entering into a covenant with God. How can we know when we're ready? Talk about the idea of starting with a covenant for a limited time period.

**Pray:** Ask the Lord to show you if there's anything hindering you from making a covenant with Him. Present that hindrance to the Lord.

FOURTEEN

# Writing Your Covenant

To make your covenant clear and memorable, I recommend that you put it in writing, date it, and file it in a place you can easily reference. You may even want to carry a printout on your person for a while. In this chapter I want to help you craft the wording of your covenant.

We're not all tempted sexually in the same way. Our covenant, therefore, needs to be individualized based on the ways we struggle personally and the triggers that activate our eye gate.

Ask the Lord to help you write a covenant that's personalized to fit your frame. If you're comfortable doing so, write it in your own words. Or, if you prefer, you're welcome to borrow from the following template.

## A SAMPLE COVENANT

The sample covenant I'm suggesting here is comprised of an introduction, a body, and a conclusion. You are welcome to follow this pattern as you write your covenant. Each of these three elements can be a sentence or longer.

Below are samples you may choose from. The introduction and conclusion are the same for everyone, but the body will vary with each individual.

## INTRODUCTION

The following introductory statement is universal. It could be used by anyone of any age:

- Heavenly Father, for the next twenty-four hours I make a covenant before You with my eyes. (Adjust the time frame as you wish.)

## BODY

For the body of your covenant, choose from the options below. Cut and paste the lines you really like, then tweak them to make the wording just right for you.

- I vow to never look upon a man/woman or picture of a man/woman to lust.
- I vow to never read sensual, suggestive, or immoral material, whether in print or electronically.
- I vow to never look at other women to determine my beauty and value.
- I will not use my eyes to flirt with anyone other than my spouse.
- I refuse to fantasize about what it would be like to be married to someone else.
- I will not allow my eyes to take a second look at a man/woman that I find attractive.
- I will not allow my eyes to take a second look at a seductive picture.
- I will not watch a movie that might have arousing scenes, and if I'm caught off guard by a movie, I will walk out or turn it off.
- I will not click on a link that might be sexually suggestive.
- I vow to never view pornography.
- I will not use sexual humor.
- I will not listen to music that is sensual or ungodly.
- I set the focus of my eyes on things above, where Christ is, sitting at the right hand God.

## CONCLUSION

I suggest your concluding statement be along these lines:

- I'm asking You to always remind me of this covenant vow I'm making with You today, and grant me the grace to always keep it. Knowing the weakness of my frame and the greatness of Your power, I throw myself upon Your mercy and strength. Amen.

## PUTTING IT TOGETHER

Putting all three components together (introduction, body, and conclusion), someone's vow might read something like this:

Heavenly Father, for the next twenty-four hours I make a covenant before You with my eyes. I vow to never let my eyes settle upon a woman to lust or compare. When I unexpectedly encounter a seductive image or a woman I'm attracted to, I will either look away, turn it off, or walk away. I set the focus of my eyes on things above, where Christ is, sitting at the right hand God. Please remind me continually of this covenant vow, and grant me the grace to keep it. Knowing the weakness of my frame and the greatness of Your power, I throw myself upon Your mercy and strength. Amen.

### [ **For Small Groups** ]

**Dig:** Underline the sample vows in this chapter that you identify with personally. Is there anything else you might want to say in your covenant with your eyes? Write down your thoughts.

**Share:** Bring all your ideas to the group, and let's help one another with the wording of our covenants, until everyone in the group has theirs written down.

**Pray:** Let's take time to pray over the declarations in our vows. Open your heart to the nearness of the Holy Spirit. Is He granting you the grace to make an eye covenant now?

## FIFTEEN

# A Wholehearted End-Time Generation

*These are the ones who were not defiled with women, for they are virgins. These are the ones who follow the Lamb wherever He goes (Rev. 14:4).*

Let me summarize the glorious advantages of making a covenant with your eyes.

1. You'll gain greater victory over lust and sin.

   If your experience is like mine, you'll notice a real, measurable, tangible difference in your victory levels related to lust. Victory over sin? You can't put a price-tag on that—it's invaluable!

2. You'll be better equipped than ever to bring "every thought into captivity to the obedience of Christ" (2 Cor. 10:5).

   Once you firmly shut the eye gate, you isolate your enemy to the outside of your castle. Now you can wrestle down your thought life from a position of advantage.

3. You'll enjoy new levels of intimacy with Jesus.

   Jesus will be enjoying you in your covenant, and you'll be able to sense it because of the tenderness of your heart. As you experience greater victory over sin, you'll become even more aware of His closeness because hindrances to love are being overcome.

4. You'll gain authority to coach an end-time generation of consecrated Nazirites.

   Revelation 14:4 describes an end-time generation of believers with a Nazirite-like devotion to Christ: "These are the ones who were not defiled with women, for they are virgins. These are the ones who follow the Lamb wherever He goes." These will have made a covenant with their eyes. Why do we know this? Because the purity they demonstrate will be attained only through an eye covenant.

Who will lead such a generation? Only those with an equally fierce commitment to purity. As you gain confidence and history in this covenant, God will turn your heart to the children coming after you (Mal. 4:6). You'll show another generation how to devote themselves in wholehearted consecration to Christ.

## A STORY

I would like to close with a story. I was traveling on a certain weekend to minister in a church, and on this particular trip I was accompanied by a young worship leader who was around twenty-five years old at the time. He's a wonderful young man, with a beautiful wife and radiant children.

We were teaming up in ministry on this particular weekend—I was the speaker, and he was the worship leader. We both lived in the same town, so we were flying together to this church.

While in the airport, as our conversation was unfolding, he said to me, "Let me tell you the prayer I pray every morning."

*Obedience opens to greater intimacy with God as hindrances to love are overcome.*

He went on to explain, "The first thing I do every morning, when my feet hit the ground, is offer a prayer to God."

Now, before I tell you his prayer, I need to give the backdrop. His prayer is based on the words of Christ, "Repent, or else I will come to you quickly and will fight against them with the sword of My mouth" (Rev. 2:16).

Jesus was speaking to the church in Pergamos, and although there were several things for which He commended them, He rebuked them because there were some in their midst who were teaching doctrine that led people into sexual immorality. Sexual immorality was being legitimatized and rationalized. Jesus sharply called them to repent of their immorality, warning them that if they didn't, He would "fight against them with the sword of [His] mouth."

I can hardly imagine anything more terrifying than having Jesus fight against you with the sword of His mouth. One day, that same sword will kill, single-handedly, the entire international army that the antichrist will assemble against Christ (Rev. 19:21). The sword of His mouth—what a dread weapon! It's this sword that my young friend had in view as he told me about his daily prayer.

He said he starts his day with this prayer:

> "Lord Jesus, if I do anything with my eyes today to violate the covenant I've made with You, I invite You to fight against me with the sword of Your mouth. But if I honor my covenant with You, and please You with the things I look upon today, I ask You to be gracious to me, bless me, and open doors of favor for me that no man can shut."

As he told me this, I just stared at him. Invoking the sword of Jesus' mouth. It was unbelievable.

As I stared at him, I didn't say it aloud, but inside I was thinking, "Who are you, anyways?"

What kind of young man prays this kind of prayer?

I'll tell you what kind. There's a generation arising in the earth in these last days that's fiercely devoted to consecration. While the world is throwing itself headlong into darkness, they're rising with an unwavering loyalty to the Lamb (Isa. 60:2). They're making covenants with their eyes. They're doing violence to the sins that want to trip and disqualify them from their inheritance in Christ. They're a Revelation 14:4

> *I can hardly imagine anything more terrifying than having Jesus fight against you with the sword of His mouth.*

generation "who were not defiled with women, for they are virgins. These are the ones who follow the Lamb wherever He goes."

The world has yet to see them.

Will you be part of this generation?

Today can be a new beginning—for *you*.

### [ For Small Groups ]

**Dig:** Spend some time meditating and praying in Revelation 14:4. Ask the Lord how you might be an undefiled virgin who follows the Lamb wherever He goes.

**Share:** Talk about the story at the end of this chapter. Look at the letter to Pergamos, Revelation 2:12-17. How does this story challenge you personally?

**Pray:** Are you willing to pray the prayer of my friend, from Revelation 2:16?

APPENDIX

# Additional Resources

The resources listed below are not included because I endorse everything they say, but because they have been recommended to me by others. Use discretion and discernment in everything you read.

The following books can be found online or at Amazon.com:

*Every Man's Battle*, by Stephen Arterburn and Fred Stoeker
*Every Young Man's Battle*, by Stephen Arterburn
*Preparing Your Son for Every Man's Battle*, by Stephen Arterburn
*Every Man's Marriage*, by Stephen Arterburn
*Every Woman's Battle*, by Shannon Ethridge and Stephen Arterburn
*The Final Freedom*, by Doug Weiss
*Get a Grip*, by Doug Weiss
*Sex, God, and Men*, by Doug Weiss
*101 Freedom Exercises*, by Doug Weiss
*Steps to Freedom*, by Doug Weiss
*Falling Forward*, by Craig Lockwood
*At the Altar of Sexual Idolatry*, by Steve Gallagher
*Pure Desire*, by Ted Roberts
*Guilt-free Living*, by Larry Jackson
*Maximized Manhood*, by Edwin Louis Cole
*The Purity Principle*, by Randy Alcorn
*Sex is not the Problem (Lust is)*, by Joshua Harris
*Winning The Battle Within*, by Neil T. Anderson
*Overcoming Sexual Sin*, by Neil T. Anderson
*False Intimacy: Understanding the Struggle of Sexual Addiction*, by Dr. Harry W. Schaumburg
*The Last Addiction*, by Sharon A. Hersh

Some sites of ministries that minister to the sexually broken:
www.purelifeministries.org
www.livingfree.org
www.newlife.com
www.sexaddict.com
www.puredesire.org
www.pureintimacy.org
www.lifecounseling.org
www.theundergroundministry.org
www.freedomeveryday.org
www.bebroken.com
www.healingforthesoul.org
www.purehope.net

Ministries that especially serve those struggling with same-sex attraction:
www.masteringlife.org
www.desertstream.org

Articles on masturbation can be found at:
http://restoringsexualpurity.org/masturbtion-its-a-form-of-false-intimacy
http://couragerc.net/Masturbation.html

Penn Clark has written a 30-day challenge for recovering personal purity, available at www.penn-clark.com/Purity/Purity/Home.html

## *All of Bob Sorge's Titles*

A COVENANT WITH MY EYES ........ $13
EXPLORING WORSHIP:
A Practical Guide to Praise & Worship ........ $16
Exploring Worship WORKBOOK & DISCUSSION GUIDE ........ $ 5
IN HIS FACE: A Prophetic Call to Renewed Focus ........ $13
THE FIRE OF DELAYED ANSWERS ........ $14
THE FIRE OF GOD'S LOVE ........ $13
PAIN, PERPLEXITY, AND PROMOTION:
A Prophetic Interpretation of the Book of Job ........ $14
DEALING WITH THE REJECTION AND PRAISE OF MAN ........ $10
GLORY: When Heaven Invades Earth ........ $10
SECRETS OF THE SECRET PLACE ........ $15
Secrets of the Secret Place: COMPANION STUDY GUIDE ........ $11
Secrets of the Secret Place: LEADER'S MANUAL ........ $ 5
ENVY: The Enemy Within ........ $12
FOLLOWING THE RIVER: A Vision for Corporate Worship ........ $10
LOYALTY: The Reach of the Noble Heart ........ $14
UNRELENTING PRAYER ........ $13
POWER OF THE BLOOD: Approaching God with Confidence ........ $13
IT'S NOT BUSINESS, IT'S PERSONAL ........ $10
OPENED FROM THE INSIDE: Taking the Stronghold of Zion ........ $11
MINUTE MEDITATIONS ........ $12
BETWEEN THE LINES: God is Writing Your Story ........ $13

*DVD Series:*
EXPLORING WORSHIP DVD SERIES ........ $30
SECRETS OF THE SECRET PLACE DVD SERIES ........ $30

*To order Bob's materials:*

- Go to www.oasishouse.com
- Call 816-767-8880 (ask about quantity discounts)
- Write Oasis House, PO Box 522, Grandview, MO 64030-0522

Go to www.oasishouse.com for special package discounts, book descriptions, ebooks, and free teachings.